How Would You Answer These Questions?

—How "long" is "long hair"?
—Does a student who is accused of cheating on an examination have a right to a hearing?
—Is a school prayer constitutional?
—Is it legal to counsel evasion of the draft?
—Can black citizens register in a hotel in any state?
—Should rioters be granted due process of law?

Now, as never before, America's citizens are asking these crucial questions. *Civil Rights and Civil Liberties* offers a penetrating analysis of the current struggle for a truly democratic and orderly society. The book also includes the Declaration of Independence, the Constitution of the United States, a summary of civil rights legislation from 1896 to 1964, and the Universal Declaration of Human Rights.

PROBLEMS OF AMERICAN SOCIETY

Focusing on the urban scene, youth, the individual and his search for a better life, the books in this series probe the most crucial dilemmas of our time.

The Negro in the City
Civil Rights and Civil Liberties
Crime and Juvenile Delinquency
Poverty and the Poor
**The City As a Community*
**Air and Water Pollution*
*City Government
*The Draft
*Slums
*The Traffic Jam
**The People of the City*
*The Consumer

*Forthcoming

BERNARD
LUDWIG

Edited by
Gerald Leinwand

Civil Rights
and
Civil Liberties

WSP WASHINGTON SQUARE PRESS   NEW YORK

CIVIL RIGHTS AND CIVIL LIBERTIES

A *Washington Square Press* edition
1st printing.....................December, 1968

Published by Washington Square Press,
a division of Simon & Schuster, Inc., 630 Fifth Avenue, New York, N.Y.

L

WASHINGTON SQUARE PRESS editions are distributed in the
U.S. by Simon & Schuster, Inc., 630 Fifth Avenue, New
York, N.Y. 10020 and in Canada by Simon & Schuster
of Canada, Ltd., Richmond Hill, Ontario, Canada.

1 2 3 4 5 1 0 9

Standard Book Number: 671-47176-7.

*To my parents
who taught me to live
in urban America*

ACKNOWLEDGMENT

This is one of a series of volumes designed to become text materials for urban schools. Partially funded under Title I, Elementary and Secondary Education Act, Public Law 89–10, 1965, the series grew out of a curriculum development project conceived and executed by the editor. Washington Square Press and the Curriculum Committee of the Trenton, New Jersey, public schools provided valuable editorial assistance.

Mrs. Bernice Munce is Project Supervisor of the Curriculum Committee which includes the following members: William Carter, Elsie Collins, Albert DeMartin, Harold P. DuShane, Barbara Hancock, Roland Hence, Steven McLaine, Gerald Popkin, Richard Scheetz, Carol West.

Also contributing to the effort were Neil O'Donnel, Joseph Fonseca and Eugene Winchester as research assistants, Mrs. Eileen Donohue as secretary, and my wife who spent hours typing and proofreading.

Preface

Few topics are so little understood as that of civil rights and civil liberties. While this volume may make a contribution to a better understanding of these problems, this preface must emphasize that what we have attempted here is but an introductory study which may raise more questions than it answers and will, in this way, prove to be but a starting point for further inquiry and investigation. It is the purpose of this book to help its readers identify and deal with some of the basic problems of our society in the area of civil rights and liberties.

Our greatest concern has been to explore current issues of civil rights and liberties—minority-group rights and those issues growing out of problems and pressures that affect young people, namely, the draft, the war in Vietnam, and the movement and attitudes of the "New Left." Among the questions we take up are the following: How shall we proceed in the struggle to achieve full equality for all under law? What is the nature of legitimate protest? What is the legitimate role, if any, of violent dissent? Is breaking the law ever justified? If so, how, when, by whom? What means for peaceful change are available?

Preface

It is not sufficient to talk about vague concepts such as liberty, freedom, and justice without looking into the complex issues that arise almost daily in the school, the community, and the nation. As the country becomes more urbanized, the rights of individuals become more difficult to preserve. The attitude that we, as individuals, are insignificant must be counteracted by a fuller understanding of how we can be heard in a society in which it is becoming increasingly difficult to hear and in which many may not wish to listen.

The essay that introduces this volume reviews some of the basic dilemmas growing out of current problems of civil rights and civil liberties. The fifteen readings that follow include significant Supreme Court decisions as well as short essays dealing with contemporary issues. It is hoped that the essay and the readings will stimulate thought, understanding, and an awareness of the uncertainties in the field of civil rights and liberties. The challenge to the reader is to use these uncertainties as a basis for further study.

Gerald Leinwand

Contents

PREFACE

PART ONE:
   Civil Rights and Civil Liberties

The Problem and the Challenge   17
How Does Our Constitution Lay the Basis for
   Civil Rights and Liberties Today?   21
What Is the Role of the United States
   Supreme Court in Relation to
   Civil Rights and Civil Liberties?   25
How Has Urbanization Influenced the Problems
   of Civil Rights?   28
How Has Youth Influenced the Civil Rights
   Movement?   31
How Has the Civil Rights Movement Affected
   the Negro Revolution?   33
How Can the Rights of Youth Be Safeguarded?   40
Should Draft-Card Burners Be Punished?   44
Is Wearing Long Hair a Civil Right?   47
How Effective Are the New Civil Rights Laws?   50

PART TWO:
   Selected Readings

   1. *The Declaration of Independence*   59
   2. *The Constitution of the United States*   62
   3. *Selected Amendments to
      the United States Constitution*   67

Contents

4. *The Right to Counsel: The Gideon Case*
   SUPREME COURT OF THE
   UNITED STATES   75
5. *Engle v. Vitale, Jr. (1962):*
   School Prayer and Religious Freedom
   by JUSTICE HUGO L. BLACK   78
6. *How Should Problems of*
   Alleged Cheating Be Handled?
   by SYDNEY H. SCHANBERG   83
7. *The Great Hair Problem*
   by SPENCER COXE   88
8. *A Call to Resist Illegitimate Authority*
   by RESIST   95
9. *Civil Disobedience*
   by BAYARD RUSTIN   102
10. *Riots in Our Cities—Newark and Beyond*
    by THE NEW YORK TIMES   107
11. *Separate but Equal: 1896–1954*
    SUPREME COURT OF THE
    UNITED STATES   112
12. *Student Reactions to the*
    Little Rock Affair of 1957
    by ANTHONY LEWIS *and*
    THE NEW YORK TIMES   119
13. *Freedom Ride Diary*
    by LOUIS E. LOMAX   126
14. *Summary of the Civil Rights Act of 1964*
    by THE NEW YORK TIMES   130
15. *The Universal Declaration of Human Rights*
    by THE UNITED NATIONS   138

PART THREE:
   Appendix

The Constitution of the United States   145

   Notes   179
   Suggestions for Additional Reading   181
   Index   183

Civil Rights
and
Civil Liberties

Part One

Civil Rights
and Civil Liberties

The Problem and the Challenge

A STUDENT is suspended from school because he does not wear the "proper" clothing. A teacher is fired because he played a record for instructional purposes which the local Board of Education believed was not "in the best interests" of the students. A young man is arrested for publicly burning his draft card. Parents picket a school because their children will be bused to another school to promote integration. A student editor of a school newspaper is suspended because he published an article severely criticizing the principal. A student is told that he must cut his hair, or else he will be suspended from school.

Headline stories such as these have become commonplace in recent years. These cases and others like them involve the rights and liberties we may or may not be allowed to have. It is very difficult to decide when and how an individual's or group's liberties are being violated or how they may be protected. How do we, as individuals and members of an organized society, determine the rights, the liberties, and the responsibilities of our fellow citizens?

Many times we answer this question by stating simply that in a democratic society the majority decides on the "proper" course of action. However, must we not protect the rights of the individual, the dissenter, the non-conformist, and members of minority groups? We believe that in our country, government and all of its agencies are the servants of the "will of the people." How do we determine the "will of the peo-

Should Police Shoot Looters?

De Facto Segregation Is a Problem of the Cities

300 STUDENTS SIT IN

City Teacher Strike

High Court to Study Draft 'Penalty'

Senate Rejects Wiretap Curb

ple?" Does majority will always protect the rights and privileges of others? These are complex issues indeed. The test that follows should emphasize the fact that the issues of civil rights and liberties lend themselves to no easy answers.

Number on a separate sheet of paper from 1 to 10 and indicate your answer by writing Y (for Yes) if you agree, or N (for No) if you do not agree.

1. Any private individual should have the right to criticize any government or government official anywhere in the world.   Y   N

2. Segregation in public schools violates the equal protection of the laws guaranteed to all Americans by the Constitution.   Y   N

3. Belonging to the Communist party should be punishable by fine or imprisonment.   Y   N

4. Religious exercises, such as The Lord's Prayer and Bible reading, should be barred from public schools.   Y   N

5. Movies, books, and plays presenting an offensive characterization of a particular racial or religious group should be suppressed.   Y   N

6. In their war against crime, policemen are entitled to listen in on private phone conversations.   Y   (N)

7. Those accused as security risks under the federal security program should have the right to confront and cross-examine their accusers.   Y   N

8. Students receiving financial aid from the government should be required to swear that they are not members of the Communist party.   Y   N

9. Racial discrimination in housing, public and private, should be prohibited by law. Y N
10. Police are entitled to hold and interrogate arrested persons as long as 24 hours before arraigning them in front of a magistrate.[1] Y N

It is probable that after you have discussed the answers to the above questions you will not always agree with your friends, parents, or teachers. Why do you not always agree on the answers? Why do you find it difficult simply to answer *yes* or *no* without qualifying your answers? Who is to decide what are the "correct" answers to these and hundreds of other questions related to these issues, all of them concerned

Many schools like this one in Englewood, New Jersey, suffer from de facto segregation for the simple reason that they are located in a ghetto area. Half of the school's Negro student body stayed home on this day to protest the system (UPI)

"It's for you."

Mike Thaler

This joke illustrates a serious controversy about the right
of law enforcement agencies to obtain evidence of a crime
by the use of electronic eavesdropping devices. Even
though a warrant must be obtained prior to such a procedure, many people argue that it is a violation of the
Fourth Amendment, which prohibits unreasonable searches
and seizures (American Civil Liberties Union)

with the protection of civil liberties and civil rights
in a free democratic society?

How Does Our Constitution Lay the Basis for Civil Rights and Liberties Today?

It is absolutely essential that you examine the document under which we, as a nation, have lived since
1788 if you want to understand the basis of our civil
rights and civil liberties. The original Constitution and
its amendments (now 25) form the legal basis under
which we can fully understand and enjoy our rights
and responsibilities as American citizens. The statement of our freedoms is often referred to as the Bill

of Rights. The Bill of Rights is the first ten amendments to the United States Constitution. They became effective on December 15, 1791, a little more than three years after the Constitution was adopted. They were added because many of the states which ratified the Constitution wanted a Bill of Rights to "restrict the power of the federal government."

In the Bill of Rights may be found the laws which assure us of freedom of speech, freedom of the press, the right to assemble peaceably, and the right to worship as we wish. Here, too, may be found the privilege that we need not testify against ourselves. Provisions for jury trial and other fair legal procedures are likewise stated. It should be remembered that although the Bill of Rights was designed to limit the power of the federal government only, much of the history of civil rights in the United States is also the story of the attempt to apply similar limits to the power of the states as well as to the power of private industry.

In addition to the Bill of Rights the body of the Constitution guarantees us certain freedoms and rights. The following protections are included:

The prohibition of any religious test for public office.

The prohibition against the suspension of the writ of *habeas corpus*—the device used to decide if a person may legally be kept in jail.

The requirement that a person be tried not in a distant place but in the state where the crime was committed.

The prohibition against *ex post facto* laws—laws which are passed today but applied to acts that were lawful yesterday.

The provisions against *bills of attainder*—laws

which bar groups of people from enjoying any rights of citizenship.

The requirement that each act of possible treason be testified to by at least two witnesses.[2]

There are other rights to protect individuals contained in more recent amendments to the Constitution:

Slavery is prohibited by the Thirteenth Amendment.

All persons born or naturalized in the United States are citizens regardless of their race or color—a right guaranteed by the Fourteenth Amendment.

No state, the Fourteenth Amendment orders, shall deprive any person of life, liberty, or property without due process of law.

The Equal Protection Clause of the Fourteenth Amendment bars any state from denying any person the equal protection of the law.

The rights of citizens to vote, says the Fifteenth Amendment, shall not be denied or abridged either by the federal government or any state on account of race or color.

A woman's right to vote is protected by the Nineteenth Amendment.

Prohibited by the Twenty-fourth Amendment is the payment of a poll tax or other tax as a qualification for voting in elections for any federal office.

The Constitution of the United States is the supreme law of the land. It is from the Constitution, as well as other federal, state, and city laws, that the individual American is guaranteed his civil rights and liberties. Any citizen or group of citizens can test in the courts the constitutionality of any law passed by any legislative body.

People today forget that women's right to vote is a relatively modern development. The Nineteenth Amendment, which gave women the vote, became part of the Constitution only after marches and demonstrations by women that were the equal of today's civil rights protests (Bettmann Archive)

It is a rather simple matter to state these almost sacred principles as proof of the guarantees of rights and liberties to all residents of our country. However, we know that what is written on paper is not necessarily what really takes place in everyday experience. Words must be brought to life by practice, experience, tradition, and, above all, interpretation. If a man owns a hotel or a restaurant, must he lodge and serve all people? Do private individuals have the right to criticize the government and/or government officials? Does segregation in public schools violate the equal protection of the law guaranteed to all Americans by the Constitution?

We turn to the courts to understand more fully how the beautiful words of our Constitution and the laws made under it may be interpreted. How do we decide when one man's freedom becomes another man's bondage? How can we protect the rights of the minority and still preserve majority rule in a democratic nation? How have the events of time and new discoveries changed the meaning of laws? Why has the Supreme Court of the United States become such an important and, at times, controversial guardian of civil rights and liberties in recent years?

What Is the Role of the United States Supreme Court in Relation to Civil Rights and Civil Liberties?

> Under our constitutional system, courts stand against any winds that blow as havens of refuge for those who might otherwise suffer because they are helpless, weak, outnumbered. . . .[3]

This statement of Justice Hugo Black has so guided Supreme Court decisions in recent years that the protection of the constitutional civil rights and civil liberties of the individual—no matter how unusual his beliefs—can accurately be described as the most important business of the Court. The Supreme Court, under Chief Justice Earl Warren, has attempted to give real meaning and effect to the commands of the Constitution and the Bill of Rights. It has received much criticism and praise for its decisions. Perhaps never has our highest Court had so great an influence on the lives of millions of Americans since the era of John Marshall (1801–1835).

The Court has delivered decisions bearing on the rights of Negroes, Communists, those too poor to hire a lawyer, those who refuse to sign loyalty oaths. It has prevented the states from admitting illegally seized evidence in trials. It has excluded forced confessions from cases heard in state courts, and it has taken major steps toward creating national uniform standards of fairness in police work.

The Supreme Court is the highest court in the land. It has been called "America's unique contribution to the theory of government." The size of the Supreme Court is fixed by Congress. At present, the Court has nine members—one chief justice and eight associate justices. The Supreme Court has *original jurisdiction* in cases affecting ambassadors and other public ministers, and in those cases to which a state is a party. Its most famous cases, however, usually involve *appellate jurisdiction*. These are cases which involve questions of the constitutionality of federal and state laws as well as cases appealed from the highest state courts. The importance of the Supreme Court is not only that there is no further appeal from its decisions, but also that its decisions are binding upon similar cases throughout the nation. In May, 1954, when the Supreme Court declared segregation in the public schools unconstitutional *(Brown v. Board of Education of Topeka),* this decision applied to all of the public schools in the United States.

The Supreme Court currently has nine members, who were appointed by four different Presidents (Franklin Roosevelt, Dwight Eisenhower, John Kennedy, and Lyndon Johnson).[4]

In June, 1967, President Lyndon Johnson appointed Thurgood Marshall to the Supreme Court. Mr. Marshall is the first Negro to serve on the bench of the Supreme Court. On June 13, 1967, *The New York Times* stated in an editorial:

> The appointment of Thurgood Marshall to the Supreme Court is rich in symbolism. Since he will be the first Negro to serve in the nation's highest

The United States Supreme Court currently has nine members, among them Thurgood Marshall, the first Negro on the Supreme Court. These Justices are not elected but appointed by the President (UPI)

tribunal, . . . Mr. Justice Marshall will be a historic figure before he ever casts a vote or drafts an opinion. It is regrettable that his appointment is historic in that special sense; but it cannot be otherwise until the United States achieves its ultimate ideal as a fully civilized, multiracial society in which race no longer matters.

Supreme Court justices are appointed for life by the President with the approval of the Senate, and they serve until retirement, death, or impeachment. One of the major criticisms of the Supreme Court is that, depending upon its membership at a given time, its decisions are too "liberal" or too "conservative." This criticism is directed particularly at decisions in cases concerned with civil rights and civil liberties. At different times in our nation's history the Supreme Court has interpreted the Constitution differently. These differences often grow out of the climate which prevails in society at any given moment. They also grow out of the ideas of the people who serve as justices. Because the Supreme Court is, in the last analysis, made up of men, it sometimes makes mistakes. But whatever its defects, the Supreme Court is the ultimate guardian of our constitutional rights and liberties. It stands at the forefront of a continuing struggle to turn into reality the ideals upon which this country was founded, and during the 1960's those realities have been changing very rapidly indeed.

How Has Urbanization Influenced the Problems of Civil Rights?

The Census Bureau estimates that by 1970 the United States will have a population of about 214 million and by 1980 a population of 260 million. Other guesses indicate a population of over 400 million by the year 2010. While the size of our total population continues to grow, so too will the movement from rural to urban areas. Nearly all future population growth in our country is expected to take place in cities. It is estimated that by the end of the century 85 percent of our population may be living in urban areas.[5]

The cities were the haven for large-scale European immigration during the nineteenth century and the first quarter of the twentieth century. Since World War I the city has become the home of a different kind of "newcomer." Negroes, Puerto Ricans, Mexican-Americans, and other groups have joined the "trek" to the city. The term ghetto, which originally meant a walled area in which the Jews of the cities of Europe were permitted to live, is now used to describe the Negro, Puerto Rican, and Mexican-American slums which exist in nearly every sizable city. Problems such as discrimination and prejudice, which lead to social tensions among and between urban groups, have developed to plague our cities and our nation.

Robert C. Weaver, former Secretary of Housing and Urban Affairs, has stated:

> There is no place in the cities of our future for ghettos of any kind—ghettos of religion or of race. The ghettos that exist must, in time, be disintegrated. In their place must be built cities open to all Americans, whatever their differences. Our goal is to . . . enable Americans to live and work together so that their differences will become the strength, rather than the weakness, of America.[6]

Of the nearly twenty-two million Negro Americans in the United States, 69 percent live in urban areas. As white people move to the suburbs, the inner city becomes largely Negro (Black Star)

Yet, in spite of such statements, ghettos and a host of related problems grow more intense year by year. Names of cities within cities continue to cause alarm and fear in the minds of millions of Americans: Watts, Harlem, Hough, Avondale, and Ybor City are synonyms for the Negro ghettos* that have developed in cities all over our nation. As Americans move closer together physically, barriers based upon the differences in race, religion, ethnic background, and economic conditions seem to grow higher.

Most Americans immediately relate any discussion of civil rights to the American Negro's struggle to achieve first-class citizenship. For a long time after slavery was abolished, Negroes continued to live in the rural South in a segregated society, but after World War I they began to migrate to the northern cities in search of jobs, better education, and dignity. After World War II the trickle begun in the 1920's became a steady stream.

Many problems develop when large groups of people come from the simple rural life into the more complicated atmosphere of the city. Tension develops in two important places: first, within and among the members of the newly arrived groups; secondly, between members of the minority group and those of the majority group. As a result, every study of civil rights must be examined within the setting of minority groups emerging from a rural way of life into a rapidly expanding and complex urban society.

One of the major dilemmas in the civil rights movement today is how we can cope with the masses of people who move from the country to a frightening

---

Negro ghettos—Watts, Los Angeles; Harlem, New York City; Hough, Cleveland; Avondale, Cincinnati; Ybor City, Tampa.

and bewildering city. How can the tensions which result from such fears be reduced? Are our traditional understandings of the meaning of civil rights and liberties changing rapidly enough to protect the newcomer among us? It has been said that one's right to swing one's arm ends where the next man's nose begins. In rural areas, where neighbors may be few and far apart, one man's rights are less likely to conflict very quickly with those of his neighbor. In the slums and ghettos of the city, however, teeming streets and overcrowded flats make it more difficult for one to do as he likes. Because in the city one's freedom is likely to conflict more readily with the freedom of others, problems of civil rights and liberties become the daily diet of man's relations with man.

How Has Youth Influenced the Civil Rights Movement?

"Revolt is necessary if we are to avoid becoming a second-rate nation."[7] Supreme Court Justice William O. Douglas, who made this remark, is one of the leaders in the movement for greater civil rights and liberties. But what does he mean by "revolt"? Does he mean revolt that would threaten to overthrow our basic institutions of government? No. He is concerned rather with revolt by the individual to encourage whatever changes are needed to meet our society's problems. Such "revolt" adds to the problems of protecting the rights and liberties of those who rebel.

In American society today there can be little doubt that the youth of the nation are in revolt. They are the rebels among us. In the fight for civil rights both the membership and leadership of many of the militant civil rights groups are drawn, for the most part, from young men and women in their twenties. Such groups as the Congress of Racial Equality (CORE), the Stu-

The majority of civil rights demonstrators are young people of college age. Evidence of youthful revolt lies in the fact that the rioters in ghettos are largely between the ages of 15 and 25 and the draft protesters are young men in their late teens and early twenties (Cecil Layne)

dent Nonviolent Coordinating Committee (SNCC), Students for a Democratic Society (SDS), and the Southern Christian Leadership Conference (SCLC) are made up of men and women of the post-World War II era who, through street marches, sit-ins, and voter-registration drives, have captured the attention of millions of Americans. Protest movements such as the "New Left," "Black Power" advocates, and groups opposing the policy of the current United States position in Vietnam have kept the issues of civil liberties under constant scrutiny.

Many attempts have been made to analyze the reasons for this "revolt." Clark Kerr, former president of the University of California and currently directing a study of higher education for the Carnegie Foundation, made this observation:

Exaggeration is one word that fits. This new generation has exaggerated itself. It has been exaggerated
by the news media. It has been exaggerated and used
by the left and the right.[8]

Attempting to explain why young people, particularly
those from middle-class, college-oriented homes, refuse
to accept the patterns and beliefs of the "older generation," Dr. Kerr points out that this generation was born
under the cloud of the A-Bomb and has become more
acutely aware of the problems of our own society and
the issues of the world through television.

Many observers felt that the late 1950's was a period
of conformity and the desire to maintain things as they
were. With the election of John F. Kennedy in 1960,
such programs of the "New Frontier" and the "Great
Society" as the Peace Corps, the war against poverty,
and the civil rights movement inflamed the imagination
and mind of many young people. The 1960's have
become a period of intense activity, notable change,
and, above all, the sometimes painful awareness that
many issues of our nation and the entire world remain
unsolved.

How Has the Civil Rights Movement Affected the Negro Revolution?

As stated earlier, every discussion of civil rights
must take into full account the struggle of the American Negro to achieve first-class citizenship. The more
than twenty million Negroes who live in the United
States represent over 11 percent of the total population. The Negro is the largest minority group in our
nation and, aside from the American Indian, has suffered the greatest amount of discrimination and perse-

Bearing the motto "Freedom Now!" the protest movement in 1963 pressed for a program of direct action. Massive marches and demonstrations protested against discrimination in labor, housing and education (Black Star)

cution. Why has there been an increased awakening to concern for the civil rights of the American Negro? Why has the current struggle in this area been called "The Second American Revolution"? How did the important Supreme Court decision of May, 1954 *(Brown v. Board of Education of Topeka),* stimulate the movement toward equal rights for the American Negro? How has the struggle for Negro rights influenced the concern for the enjoyment of civil liberties by all Americans?

Although the struggle to achieve civil rights for the Negro began many years before 1954, the impact of the Supreme Court decision of that year has had a tremendous and perhaps decisive impact upon the "Negro revolution."

Between 1896 and 1954 legal segregation was an accepted pattern of American life in almost one-third of our nation. Even though the *Plessy v. Ferguson* decision of 1896 applied only to transportation, it was assumed that all other aspects of American life were included. The doctrine of "separate but equal" facilities became a way of life accepted by most Negroes and whites in the North as well as in the South.

Plessy v. Ferguson stemmed from a Louisiana law (1890) which provided that "all railway companies carrying passengers in their coaches in this state shall provide equal but separate accommodations for the white and the colored races. . . ." Plessy had refused to move from the seat he occupied in the white compartment of a railroad car and was arrested for thus violating the law. The Supreme Court, by a vote of seven to one, found the Louisiana law constitutional. Associate Justice Henry Billings Brown delivered the majority opinion of the Court. In upholding the law, he wrote, "If the two races are to meet on terms of social equality, it must be the result of . . . a mutual appreciation of each other's merits and a voluntary consent of individuals."[9]

One dissenter from this decision foreshadowed in many respects the Brown decision of fifty-eight years later. In the following statements Justice John Marshall Harlan predicted the trend of the future in race relations:

> The destinies of the two races in this country are indissolubly linked together, and the interests of both require that the common government of all shall not permit the seeds of race hate to be planted under the sanction of law.[10]

"Our Constitution is color-blind," continued Justice Harlan, "and neither knows nor tolerates classes among citizens."

Fifty-eight years later, Chief Justice Earl Warren, speaking for the unanimous decision, stated that in the field of public education the doctrine of "separate but equal" had no place. He stated it very clearly:

> Does segregation of children in public schools solely on the basis of race, even though the physical facilities and other "tangible" factors may be equal, deprive these children of the minority group of equal educational opportunities? We believe it does.[11]

This important Supreme Court decision served to mobilize the forces in both the Negro and the white communities to fight through legal means and moral persuasion to end segregation in all areas of American society. New organizations joined—and at other times fought—the older groups to secure the rights and free-

Demonstrators gather outside Democratic National Headquarters in downtown Chicago during the 1968 convention (Wide World)

doms of the American Negro. Such groups as the Congress of Racial Equality, the Southern Christian Leadership Conference, and the Student Nonviolent Coordinating Committee became prominent along with the older and more established National Association for the Advancement of Colored People (NAACP) and the Urban League. Prominent names in the struggle for equal rights included Rev. Ralph Abernathy, Julian Bond, A. Rap Brown, Stokely Carmichael, Medgar Evers, James Farmer, the late Martin Luther King, Jr., Floyd McKissick, James Meredith, A. Philip Randolph, Bayard Rustin, Rev. Fred Shuttlesworth, Roy Wilkins, and Whitney Young.

During the past ten or more years many problems and frustrations have developed in the cause of civil rights. Where do we begin to redress the grievances of people who, for the most part, have been downtrodden for several hundred years? How do we cope with the "backlash" that has developed among many whites throughout the nation? How do we change the traditions of segregation that have become part of all of our institutions? What methods should be employed by the various civil rights groups? In what areas do we begin to break down the barriers of a segregated society? How do we "compensate" the Negro for the injury he has suffered? How do we prevent violence,

39

(Bill Mauldin)

riot, and hatred that continue and will continue to break out in city after city throughout the nation? How do we remove the scars of segregation from our society without destroying that society's very fabric?

How Can the Rights of Youth Be Safeguarded?

Most people believe that there should be special ways of treating young people when they become involved in law violations. In most states, cities, and local communities, special courts and, at times, special procedures are used in dealing with juveniles. Yet on May 14, 1967, the Supreme Court made a decision stating that juvenile courts must grant young people the same rights in court procedures as are required by the Bill

The Report of the National Advisory Commission on Civil Disorders, made public in 1968, revealed that riots in cities such as Newark during the previous summer were ignited by people suffering from bad housing, underemployment, and poor representation in government (Wide World)

of Rights in adult trials. According to *The New York Times* of May 15, 1967, "the landmark decision is expected to require that radical changes be made immediately in most of the nation's 3,000 juvenile courts."[12]

Justice Abe Fortas, who wrote the majority opinion (Justice Stewart was the only dissenter), stated that in delinquency hearings before juvenile court judges, children must be accorded the following safeguards of the Bill of Rights:

1. Timely notice of the charges against them.
2. The right to have a lawyer, appointed by the court if necessary.
3. The right to confront and cross-examine complainants and other witnesses.
4. Adequate warning of the privilege of refusing to testify against himself and of the right to remain silent.

This decision can have a tremendous impact upon our legal system as well as upon our educational system. Most people believe that young people should receive guidance and protection from their parents, teachers, and from society in general. Americans believe that one of the main functions of our educational system is to train our young people to grow up to be "good citizens." Where do we draw the line and say that not only should young people *learn* about the Bill of Rights but also have the right to exercise these rights? If we are to give young people their rights, must they not also accept the responsibilities that go along with the rights?

It is extremely important that in a free society young people should receive instruction, training, and practice in developing a working knowledge of the civil liberties to which they and others are entitled. Certainly parents

This demonstration by the young members of the Committee for a Sane Nuclear Policy is an example of the increased public awareness of the ability of public opinion to influence government policies (UPI)

and teachers have a crucial role in setting the example for the young. However, young people must also come to grips with those daily problems which involve their rights and responsibilities as well as those of others. Do we permit dissent in our classroom discussions? Do we respect the opinions of others even though we may not always agree? Do we try to understand the feelings and attitudes of people who may be different from us? How do we arrive at decisions in our clubs or student council or other organizations or groups of which we may be members?

Justice Harold R. Medina, a federal senior circuit judge, perhaps has the beginnings of an answer to these questions.

43

Young people now in school need not be cynical or adopt a "What can I do?" attitude. They can begin by understanding the Bill of Rights. Then they can jump in to defend these rights whenever necessary.

If students start doing these things now, when they become adult citizens they will not be wafted this way and that by every whim. They will have some lasting, durable principles with which to meet every challenge to our basic American liberties.[13]

In the spirit of Justice Medina's statement, the following two issues are presented for study, discussion, and analysis.

Should Draft-Card Burners Be Punished?

One of the newer forms of protest has been the public burning of draft cards by young men who have registered, as required by federal law, under the Selective Service System at the local draft boards. All eighteen-year-olds receive a "draft registration card" which they must carry with them at all times. In recent months various individuals have publicly burned their draft cards in order to exhibit their disapproval of the draft and/or United States policy in Vietnam. For this action many of these individuals have been arrested, convicted, and sentenced by federal judges and juries.

Although highly publicized, these incidents are very rare. Nevertheless, they do involve the question of individual rights. How does an individual demonstrate his opposition to policies and laws he opposes? When is protest no longer legitimate?

The entire issue of draft-card burning may eventually be decided by the United States Supreme Court. The

Opposition to the war in Vietnam prompted many young men of draft age to burn their draft cards as a symbol of their disapproval of United States presence in that country. This act is punishable as a federal offense (UPI)

Some people feel that draft-card burning is an objectionable way of expressing opposition to the Vietnam war. Many lawsuits have been brought in an effort to get the Supreme Court to decide the legality of such a protest. Other people strongly recommend a complete overhaul of the present draft system (UPI)

American Civil Liberties Union and the New York Civil Liberties Union have defended people who have been convicted of burning their draft cards. Their position is that the 1965 amendment to the Selective Service Act which seeks to punish anyone who knowingly destroys or mutilates a Selective Service certificate is unconstitutional as a limitation on the right of free expression.

> In singling out persons engaged in protest for special treatment, the Amendment strikes at the very core of what the First Amendment protects. It has long been beyond doubt that symbolic action may be protected by speech.[14]

On the other hand, the United States Court of Appeals for the Second Circuit affirmed a draft-card burning conviction and denied that draft-card burning was symbolic speech protected by the First Amendment. The Court said:

> We conclude that forbidding destruction of Selective Service certificates serves legitimate purposes in administering the system. . . . We find that the statute is neither arbitrary nor without purpose, that it is reasonably related to the power of Congress to raise and support armies, and that it reinforces an obligation which has been imposed upon registrants for many years. Accordingly, the judgment of conviction is affirmed.[15]

With which of the above positions do you agree in this matter of draft-card burning? Ultimately it will be up to the courts, perhaps even to the Supreme Court, to decide the issue.

Is Wearing Long Hair a Civil Right?

From all over the country stories of students being suspended from school and of legal action in their behalf being taken by parents and students have appeared in newspapers, magazines, television, and radio. Headline stories involving "long hair," "granny dresses," "miniskirts," and even the wearing of a skullcap by an Orthodox Jewish boy have caused much discussion and controversy. On August 9, 1967, a story was carried in *The New York Times* about the expulsion of a boy from a Hillside, New Jersey, summer school for wearing a skullcap (*yarmulke*) to his classes. The boy's father stated that "the rights of my son to practice his religion have been violated."[16] The president of the Board of Education said that he would seek a ruling on this issue from the New Jersey State Commissioner of Education.

The problem of student dress and personal appearance and the school's right to regulate them is not very uncommon and is a source of much difficulty. In October, 1966, two boys in a New York City high school complained to the New York Civil Liberties Union that they had been punished because the principal found their hair too long. The boys claimed that they were separated from the classes and confined to a wooden bench in the dean's office. They had been given their study assignments but were forbidden to discuss their lessons with their teachers. Backed by the New York Civil Liberties Union, the two students appealed to the New York State Commissioner of Education. The result was that the superintendent of the New York City schools returned the boys to their classes.[17]

Years ago it was almost unheard of for students to

This billboard appeared in Norwalk, Connecticut, where four students were suspended from school because they had long hair (UPI)

make civil liberties cases out of rules and regulations made by school officials. Now such cases have become more common, and the publicity has grown in proportion.

Most school officials argue that the relationship of the school to the student is that of *"in loco parentis"* (in place of the parent). They believe that it is both absurd and disruptive to attempt to make civil liberties cases out of the enforcement of school regulations. Mr. Fred Hechinger, Education Editor of *The New York Times,* states that the schoolmen's claim is that dress regulations have a place in the educational scheme. He continues by explaining that "if schooling is to make the graduate generally presentable, let alone employable, then such regulations are legitimate." Mr. Hechinger concludes his analysis of this issue with the following statement:

A good principal gives pupils the benefit of a hearing, but this does not imply any legal claim to

OF NORWALK

BEAUTIFY AMERICA

get a
haircut

Alan T. Pearce

"due process" nor the right to invoke the Fifth Amendment. If a student walks around town with a swastika, this is his civil right. But a principal's ban of such insignia on campus would hardly constitute a violation of the student's civil liberties, even if no classmate or teacher took offense.[19]

On the other hand, does the suspension or expulsion of students for "improper dress" violate the individual rights and academic freedom of students? Who should determine what is proper dress in a school situation? How "long" is "long hair"? How short are "short skirts"? It is very difficult to arrive at answers that will be satisfactory to all parties involved. How would you decide the answers to these questions? Have you taken into consideration the points of view of students, school officials, parents, and the community as a whole?

In conclusion, the goal we should attempt to achieve in the area of civil liberties has been well expressed by Associate Justice William J. Brennan, Jr.

Ours is a nation of many divergent groups. In one way or another each of us at some time is a member of a "minority group." But our differences can't hide the fact that we are all Americans who live under a Constitution which is blind to any differences in our rights and privileges because of race, religion, or national ancestry.[20]

How Effective Are the New Civil Rights Laws?

Most civil rights leaders believe that one of the main struggles is to persuade the United States Congress to pass civil rights legislation. For many years passage of such laws had been effectively blocked by a determined group of southern senators, although two civil rights laws were passed in 1957 and 1960. After a wave of militancy had swept across America during the spring and summer of 1963, President Kennedy began to mobilize support for the enactment of civil rights legislation. In a message to Congress, he stated:

There are no "white" and "colored" signs on the fox holes or graveyards of battle. Surely, in 1963, one hundred years after emancipation, it should not be necessary for any American citizen to demonstrate in the streets for the opportunity to stop at a hotel, or to eat at a lunch counter in the very same department store in which he is shopping, or to enter a motion picture house on the same terms as any other customer. Many Negro children entering segregated grade schools at the same time of the Supreme Court decision of 1954 will enter segregated high schools this year, having suffered a loss which can never be regained. Indeed, discrimination in education is one basic cause of the other inequities and hardships inflicted upon our Negro citizens.[21]

These children are attending a "Freedom School" set up to protest de facto segregation. Even after the Civil Rights Act of 1964 such "unofficial" segregation still exists in schools, employment and housing (UPI)

Not until July 2, 1964, was the bill signed into law by President Johnson.

To many, the passage of this law was a landmark in a long struggle. The Civil Rights Act of 1964 forbade racial discrimination in the use of publicly owned or operated facilities and in most places of public accommodation. It authorized the Attorney General to work in behalf of persons who experienced the lash of discrimination. It prohibited voting registrars from applying different standards to white and Negro applicants. It forbade discrimination in employment, union membership, and federally aided programs. It authorized the establishment of two new federal agencies—

a commission to investigate allegations of discrimination by employers or unions, and a community-relations service in the Department of Commerce to help conciliate racial disputes. The act also extended the life of the Civil Rights Commission to January 31, 1968.

In 1965 the Congress passed and the President signed a Voting Rights Bill. The act suspended the use of literacy or other voter-qualification tests, authorized the appointment of federal voting examiners for Negro registration in areas not meeting certain voter participation requirements, and provided for federal initiation of court suits to bar discriminatory poll taxes.

Before signing the Bill on August 6, 1965, President Johnson went to the rotunda of the Capitol. Standing before a statue of Abraham Lincoln, he said:

> Today the Negro story and the American story fuse and blend. This good Congress acted swiftly in passing this act. I intend to act with equal dispatch

For many years Negroes were prevented from voting by poll taxes, impossible literacy tests and endlessly detailed forms. Finally after the Voting Rights Act was passed in 1965, these restrictions were abolished and thousands of Negroes registered to vote for the first time (Wide World)

in enforcing it. If any county anywhere in this nation does not want federal intervention, it need only open its polling places to all of its people. Let me now say to every Negro in this country, "You must register. You must vote. You must learn, so that your choice advances your interest and the interest of our beloved nation. Negro leaders should respond to the Act's great challenge not simply by protests and demonstrations but by working around the clock to teach people their responsibilities."[22]

The civil rights leaders who hailed the passage of the civil rights laws of 1964 and 1965 know that laws alone will not change prejudices that have developed over the years. They recognize that no laws will smash down the walls of segregated slums or erase the inherited handicaps of undereducation and poverty. Laws will not and cannot create new and better-paying jobs in an era when automation is eliminating tens of

In many areas, North and South, white people abide by the Civil Rights Act but do not like it. When the act was passed by Congress in 1964 some public school systems closed rather than comply with the law (Stan Wayman—Urban League)

thousands of unskilled jobs. Progress has been made, but racism continues to plague those who believe in integrated American society.

Many studies have been made about whether the civil rights movement is moving too slowly or too fast. Some feel that only through education can a truly integrated society emerge; others advocate more legislative action on the federal, state, and local levels; and some Negro leaders believe that "black power" is the only real road to success. At the end of their study entitled *The Negro Revolution in America,* William Brink and Louis Harris note the attitude of Negroes toward progress in the civil rights movement.[23]

	Total Rank and File %	% Non-South	% South	% Leaders
Too slow	51	57	46	77
About right	31	32	32	20
Too fast	3	2	3	1
Not sure	15	9	19	2

The authors conclude their study with the following short interview:

> Susie Hazzard, a maid in suburban Cleveland, spoke for her people in a few words: "I want some of those flowers before I die—give me some of my flowers while I live."[24]

The "flowers" of civil rights and liberties belong to white as well as black, to young as well as old. But like flowers, civil rights require constant care and nourishment.

Part Two

Selected Readings

Written in 1776, the American Declaration of Independence has long been regarded as the source of inspiration for revolution the world over. Although designed to state the American position against England, it also provided a new structure upon which to base popular government. Why is this document regarded as a revolutionary statement? Is the Declaration of Independence still relevant?

1. The Declaration of Independence

WHEN in the Course of human events, it becomes necessary for one people to dissolve the political bands which have connected them with another, and to assume among the powers of the earth, the separate and equal station to which the Laws of Nature and of Nature's God entitle them, a decent respect to the opinions of mankind requires that they should declare the causes which impel them to the separation.

We hold these truths to be self-evident, that all men are created equal, that they are endowed by their Creator with certain unalienable Rights,* that among these are Life, Liberty, and the pursuit of Happiness. That to secure these rights, Governments are instituted among Men, deriving their just powers from the con-

---

endowed . . . unalienable Rights—given rights which belong to each human being.

sent of the governed; that whenever any Form of Government becomes destructive of these ends, it is the Right of the People to alter or to abolish it, and to institute new Government, laying its foundation on such principles and organizing its powers in such form, as to them shall seem most likely to effect their Safety and Happiness. Prudence, indeed, will dictate that Governments long established should not be changed for light and transient causes;* and accordingly all experience hath shown, that mankind are more disposed to suffer, while evils are sufferable, than to right themselves by abolishing the forms to which they are accustomed. But when a long train of abuses and usurpations,* pursuing invariably the same Object evinces a design to reduce them under absolute Despotism,* it is their right, it is their duty, to throw off such Government and to provide new Guards for their future security . . .

We, therefore . . . solemnly publish and declare, That these United Colonies are, and of Right ought to be, Free and Independent States. . . .

FURTHER INQUIRY

1. To what extent do you regard it true or false "that all men are created equal"?
2. On what grounds can a people abolish a government it believes no longer serves its purpose?
3. Does the Declaration of Independence approve the violent overthrow of a government?

---

transient causes—causes which pass quickly and therefore are meaningless in the total life of a nation.

usurpations—taking powers or rights by force.

absolute Despotism—government by one man whose word is law.

In this reading we reproduce those portions of the main part of the Constitution itself which contain many of the safeguards of our civil rights and liberties. The Constitution in full is printed in the appendix to this volume and, by referring to it, you will see how these portions of the Constitution relate to the rest of the document. How do these provisions safeguard our civil rights and liberties?

2. The Constitution of the United States

(ARTICLE 1, Section 9, Clause 2). The Privilege of the Writ of Habeas Corpus* shall not be suspended, unless when in cases of Rebellion or Invasion the public safety may require it.

(Article 1, Section 9, Clause 3). No Bill of Attainder* or Ex-Post Facto Law* shall be passed.

Writ of Habeas Corpus—a court order forcing the authorities to bring a person into open court without delay and to prove that there are legal reasons for holding him in custody.

Bill of Attainder—a law providing for punishment of an individual without a trial.

Ex-Post Facto Law—a law which makes a person liable to punishment for an act which was not considered a crime at the time it was committed.

(Article III, Section 1, Clause 1). The judicial Power* of the United States, shall be vested in one supreme Court, and in such inferior Courts as the Congress may from time to time ordain and establish.

(Article III, Section 1, Clause 2). The judges, both of the supreme and inferior Courts, shall hold their Offices during good Behavior, and shall, at stated times, receive for their Services, a Compensation which shall not be diminished during their Continuance in office.

(Article III, Section 2, Clause 3). The Trial of all Crimes, except in Cases of Impeachment,* shall be by Jury; and such Trial shall be held in the State where the said Crimes shall have been committed; but when not committed within any State, the Trial shall be at such Place or Places as the Congress may by Law have directed.

(Article III, Section 3, Clause 1). Treason against the United States, shall consist only in levying War against them, or in adhering to their Enemies, giving them Aid and Comfort. No person shall be convicted of Treason unless on the Testimony of two Witnesses to the same overt Act, or on Confession in open Court.

(Article VI, Clause 3). The Senators and Representatives before mentioned, and the Members of the several State Legislatures, and all executive and judicial Officers, both of the United States and of the several States, shall be bound by Oath or Affirmation, to support this Constitution; but no religious Test shall ever be required as a Qualification to any Office or public Trust under the United States.

--- ----

judicial Power—matters dealing with law and the courts.

Impeachment—charging a public figure with wrongdoing.

Many legal safeguards protect the rights of those arrested. Certain groups, like the American Civil Liberties Union and the National Association for the Advancement of Colored People shown here, have battled to ensure these rights for underprivileged people (Wide World)

Everyone accused of a crime in this country is presumed innocent until it is proved otherwise. Much time is spent trying to select an impartial jury and the press is often reminded not to try the defendant in the news media. The defendant is told that he does not have to give evidence that would incriminate him (UPI)

FURTHER INQUIRY

1. Why is the privilege of the writ of habeas corpus so important?
2. Why is the Congress forbidden to pass a bill of attainder or ex-post facto laws?
3. Why must all congressmen, state legislators, executive and judicial officers of the states swear to uphold the Constitution?

Although the first ten amendments contain many of our basic rights, other additions (amendments) to the Constitution have reinforced and extended those rights. Reproduced here are the more important ones. The amendments may also be found in the appendix to this volume, where they are incorporated, as they must be, with the Constitution itself.

Consider: How can the rights listed in the Bill of Rights be guaranteed to all citizens?

3. Selected Amendments to the United States Constitution

AMENDMENT I. Congress shall make no law respecting an establishment of religion, or prohibiting the free exercise thereof; or abridging the freedom of speech, or of the press; or the right of the people peaceably to assemble, and to petition the Government for a redress of grievances.*

AMENDMENT II. A well regulated Militia, being necessary to the security of a free State, the right of the people to keep and bear Arms, shall not be infringed.*

---

redress of grievances—a correction of wrongs.

infringed—trampled upon, violated.

The best-known section of our Constitution is the Bill of
Rights, which includes the first ten amendments. The First
Amendment guarantees the right of American people to
gather peacefully in any cause (UPI)

AMENDMENT III. No Soldier shall, in time of peace be quartered* in any house, without the consent of the Owner, nor in time of war, but in a manner to be prescribed by law.

AMENDMENT IV. The right of the people to be secure in their persons, houses, papers, and effects, against unreasonable searches and seizures, shall not be violated, and no Warrants* shall issue, but upon probable cause, supported by Oath or affirmation, and particularly describing the place to be searched, and the persons or things to be seized.

AMENDMENT V. No person shall be held to answer for a capital* or otherwise infamous crime, unless on a presentment or indictment of a Grand Jury,* except in cases arising in the land or naval forces, or in the Militia, when in actual service in time of War or public danger; nor shall any person be subject for the same offence to be twice put in jeopardy of life or limb; nor shall be compelled in any criminal case to be a witness against himself nor be deprived of life, liberty, or property, without due process of law; nor shall private property be taken for public use, without just compensation.

AMENDMENT VI. In all criminal prosecutions, the accused shall enjoy the right to a speedy and public trial, by an impartial jury of the State and district wherein the crime shall have been committed, which

---

quartered—stationed.

Warrants—documents giving authority.

capital—punishable by death.

Grand Jury—a jury composed of from 12 to 23 citizens set up to decide whether there is sufficient evidence to warrant an indictment, *i.e.*, a charge or accusation.

The National Guard formed under the conditions of the Second Amendment can be activated by the governor of the state to which it belongs. National guardsmen have been called out often in recent years to quell riots as these men are doing in Cleveland, Ohio (Wide World)

district shall have been previously ascertained by law, and to be informed of the nature and cause of the accusation; to be confronted with the witnesses against him; to have compulsory process for obtaining witnesses in his favor, and to have the Assistance of Counsel for his defense.

AMENDMENT VII. In Suits at common law, where the value in controversy shall exceed twenty dollars, the right of trial by jury shall be preserved, and no fact tried by a jury, shall be otherwise reexamined in any Court of the United States, than according to the rules of the common law.

AMENDMENT VIII. Excessive bail* shall not be re-

bail—a kind of cash deposit posted for the temporary release of prisoners from jail while awaiting trial.

A national furor arose in July, 1967, when state police and national guardsmen searched homes in the Negro ghetto of Plainfield, New Jersey, for 46 stolen guns. Under the Fourth Amendment people are protected from unreasonable searches and seizures (UPI)

quired, nor excessive fines imposed, nor cruel and unusual punishments inflicted.

AMENDMENT IX. The enumeration in the Constitution, of certain rights, shall not be construed to deny or disparage others retained by the people.

AMENDMENT X. The Powers not delegated to the United States by the Constitution, nor prohibited by it to the States, are reserved to the States respectively, or to the people.

AMENDMENT XIII, Section 1 (Approved December 18, 1865). Neither slavery nor involuntary servitude, except as a punishment for crime whereof the party shall have been duly convicted, shall exist within the United States, or any place subject to their jurisdiction.

AMENDMENT XIV, Section 1 (Approved July 23, 1868). All persons born or naturalized in the United States and subject thereof, are citizens of the United States and of the State wherein they reside. No State shall make or enforce any law which shall abridge the privileges or immunities* of citizens of the United States; nor shall any State deprive any person of life, liberty, or property, without due process of law; nor deny to any person within its jurisdiction the equal protection of the laws.

AMENDMENT XV, Section 1 (Approved March 30, 1870). The right of citizens of the United States to vote shall not be denied or abridged by the United States or by any State on account of race, color, or previous condition of servitude.

AMENDMENT XIX, Clause 1 (Approved August 26, 1920). The right of citizens of the United States to

---

immunities—protections.

This man from Batesville, Mississippi, reported to be 106 years old, has registered to vote for the first time in his life. Although the right to vote was guaranteed to all men by the Fifteenth Amendment in 1870, almost a hundred years passed before southern Negroes could easily take part in elections (Wide World)

vote shall not be denied or abridged by the United States or by any State on account of sex.

AMENDMENT XXIV, Section 1 (Approved January 23, 1964). The right of citizens of the United States to vote in any primary* or other election for President

---

primary election—an election within a political party which determines which candidates will run for office on election day.

or Vice President, for electors* for President or Vice President, or for Senator or Representative in Congress, shall not be denied or abridged by the United States or any State by reason of failure to pay any poll tax* or other tax.

FURTHER INQUIRY

1. Why are the first ten amendments called the "Bill of Rights"?
2. How do each of the amendments listed help to guarantee our civil rights and civil liberties?
3. Why is it necessary for the courts to interpret these amendments?

electors—members of the Electoral College. In a presidential election, the voter does not vote directly for President or Vice President. When the voter pulls the lever down, he votes for members of a group of people called electors. The "Electoral College" will in turn vote for the President and Vice President.

poll tax—a tax paid in order to vote.

On August 4, 1961, Clarence Earl Gideon allegedly broke into a poolroom in Panama City, Florida, and was caught by the police. When brought to court, he said he could not pay for a lawyer and asked the court to appoint one for him. The court said that it could not do so since he was not being accused of a crime punishable by death. Gideon held that the Supreme Court had ruled that he was entitled to a lawyer. The trial took place, Gideon had no lawyer, and was found guilty. Gideon appealed, in a handwritten note, to the United States Supreme Court. What follows is what the Supreme Court decided in a unanimous decision. What significance may be attached to this decision?

4. The Right to Counsel: The Gideon Case

SUPREME COURT OF THE UNITED STATES

NOT only these precedents but also reason and reflection require us to recognize that in our . . . system of criminal justice, any person haled into court, who is too poor to hire a lawyer, cannot be assured a fair trial unless counsel is provided for him.

This seems to us to be an obvious truth. Governments, both state and federal, quite properly spend vast sums of money to establish machinery to try defen-

From *Liberty Under Law,* published by American Education Publications, Inc., Education Center, Columbus, Ohio (1963), pp. 47–50. Copyright © 1967 by American Education Publications, a Xerox company.

In 1963 the Supreme Court handed down what is commonly called the Gideon decision. Clarence Gideon, convicted in 1961 on a felony charge, appealed his conviction on the grounds that he was refused legal counsel because he could not afford to pay for it. The Supreme Court decreed that every citizen is entitled to counsel (Wide World)

dants accused of crime. Lawyers to prosecute* are everywhere deemed essential to protect the public's interest in an orderly society.

Similarly, there are few defendants charged with crime, few indeed, who fail to hire the best lawyers they can get to prepare and present their defenses. That government hires lawyers to prosecute and defendants who have the money hire lawyers to defend are the strongest indications of the widespread belief that lawyers in criminal courts are necessities, not luxuries. The right of one charged with crime to counsel may not be deemed fundamental and essential to fair trials in some countries, but it is in ours.

From the very beginning, our state and national Constitutions and laws have laid great emphasis on procedural and substantive safeguards designed to assure fair trials before impartial tribunals in which every defendant stands equal before the law. This noble ideal cannot be realized if the poor man charged with crime

---

prosecute—press charges in a legal manner.

has to face his accusers without a lawyer to assist him. A defendant's need for a lawyer is nowhere better stated than in the moving words of Mr. Justice Sutherland:

"The right to be heard would be, in many cases, of little avail if it did not comprehend the right to be heard by counsel. Even the intelligent and educated layman has small and sometimes no skill in the science of the law.

"If charged with crime, he is incapable, generally, of determining for himself whether the indictment* is good or bad. He is unfamiliar with the rules of evidence.

"Left without the aid of counsel he may be put on trial without a proper charge, and convicted upon incompetent evidence, or evidence irrelevant to the issue or otherwise inadmissible. He lacks both the skill and knowledge adequately to prepare his defense, even though he may have a perfect one. He requires the guiding hand of counsel at every step in the proceedings against him."

The judgment is reversed and the case is remanded to the Supreme Court of Florida* for further action not inconsistent with this opinion.

FURTHER INQUIRY

1. Can a trial be fair if the accused has no lawyer to defend him? Give reasons for your point of view.
2. Do the rich have a better chance to obtain justice than the poor? Explain.

---

indictment—charge.

remanded to the Supreme Court of Florida—send the case back to the court. In the new trial, in August, 1963, Gideon was found not guilty.

"Almighty God, we acknowledge our dependence upon Thee, and we beg Thy blessings upon us, our parents, our teachers and our country." This prayer was urged by the Board of Regents of the State of New York for daily recital by pupils in the schools of the state at the opening of each school day. Parents of a number of pupils challenged the use of an official prayer and eventually the case reached the United States Supreme Court, where Justice Black delivered the majority opinion. The excerpt below is from that opinion. It is followed by a dissenting opinion. Does religion have a place in schools?

*5. Engle v. Vitale, Jr. (1962): School Prayer and Religious Freedom

by JUSTICE HUGO L. BLACK
Supreme Court of the United States

IT is neither sacrilegious* nor antireligion to say that each separate government in this country should stay out of the business of writing or sanctioning official prayers* and leave that purely religious function to the people themselves.

It is a matter of history that this very practice of establishing governmentally composed prayers for reli-

---

sacrilegious—the violation of something held sacred.

sanctioning official prayers—writing or approving an *official* prayer. Note the emphasis here on the fact that the court frowned on this practice.

From *The United States Constitution in Perspective,* by Claude L. Heathcock (Boston: Allyn and Bacon, Inc., 1964), pp. 292–293.

gious services was one of the reasons which caused
many of our early colonists to leave England and seek
religious freedom in America.

The First Amendment was added to the Constitution to stand as a guarantee that neither the power nor
the prestige of the Federal Government would be used
to control, support or influence the kinds of prayer
the American people can say—that the people's reli-
gions must not be subjected to the pressures of government for change each time a new political administra-
tion is elected to office.

Under the Amendment's prohibition against government establishment of religion, as reinforced by the
provisions of the Fourteenth Amendment,* government
of this country, be it State or federal, is without power
to prescribe by law any particular form of prayer which
is to be used as an official prayer in carrying on any
program of governmentally sponsored religious activity.

Mr. Justice Stewart, dissenting.

. . . The Court does not hold, nor could it, that New
York has interfered with the free exercise of anybody's
religion. For the state courts have made clear that
those who object to reciting the prayer must be entirely free of any compulsion to do so, including any
"embarrassments and pressures." But the Court says
that in permitting school children to say this simple
prayer, the New York authorities have established an
"official religion."

Fourteenth Amendment—largely expands the Bill of Rights
(Amendments I to X) so that most, not all, of its provisions apply to the states as well. (See amendments in
the appendix.)

From *American Constitutional Law*, by Rocco J. Tresolini (New
York: The Macmillan Company, 1965), pp. 480–481.

With all respect, I think the Court has misapplied a great constitutional principle. I cannot see how an "official religion" is established by letting those who want to say a prayer say it. On the contrary, I think that to deny the wish of these school children to join in reciting this prayer is to deny them the opportunity of sharing in the spiritual heritage of our Nation. . . .

At the opening of each day's Session of this Court we stand, while one of our officials invokes the protection of God. Since the days of John Marshall our Crier has said, "God save the United States and this Honorable Court." Both the Senate and the House of Representatives open their daily Sessions with prayer. Each of our Presidents, from George Washington to John F. Kennedy, has upon assuming his Office asked the protection and the help of God.

A year after the Supreme Court decision, second graders in the Robert Frost School in Lawrence, Mass., bow their heads in prayer in memory of the poet who died that morning (Wide World)

The Court today says that the states and federal governments are without constitutional power to prescribe any particular form of words to be recited by any group of the American people on any subject touching religion. The third stanza of "The Star-Spangled Banner," made our National Anthem by Act of Congress in 1931, contains these verses:

> "Blest with victory and peace, may the
>   heav'n rescued land
> Praise the Pow'r that hath made and
>   preserved us a nation!
> Then conquer we must when our cause it
>   is just,
> And this be our motto, 'In God is our
>   Trust.' "

81

In 1954 Congress added a phrase to the Pledge of Allegiance to the Flag so that it now contains the words "one Nation under God, indivisible, with liberty and justice for all." In 1952 Congress enacted legislation calling upon the President each year to proclaim a National Day of Prayer. Since 1865 the words "In God We Trust" have been impressed on our coins.

Countless similar examples could be listed, but there is no need to belabor the obvious. . . .

I do not believe that this Court, or the Congress, or the President has by the actions and practices I have mentioned established an "official religion" in violation of the Constitution. And I do not believe the State of New York has done so in this case. What each has done has been to recognize and to follow the deeply entrenched and highly cherished spiritual traditions of our Nation—traditions which come down to us from those who almost 200 years ago avowed their "firm reliance on the Protection of Divine Providence" when they proclaimed the freedom and independence of this brave new world.

I dissent.

FURTHER INQUIRY

1. If you were a member of the Supreme Court would you concur in the majority view? Why or why not?
2. To what extent do you agree or disagree with the reasoning of the Court as presented above?
3. If each pupil were to write a prayer of his own choosing, would the court approve?

The following reading is an account of a case involving a high school girl from Flushing, New York. It is significant to students throughout the country because it focuses on the basic question of the rights of teenagers when accused. Do you think that minors should be granted the same rights to due process of law as adults?

6. How Should Problems of Alleged Cheating Be Handled?

by SYDNEY H. SCHANBERG

A HIGH SCHOOL STUDENT charged with cheating on a State Regents examination cannot have his Regents privileges revoked—and thus be effectively barred from college—without being allowed to defend himself at a hearing with the aid of counsel, a State Supreme Court justice has ruled.

Justice Lester Holtzman, in a decision handed down in Queens Supreme Court last week, held that a girl student, by being denied a proper hearing, had been deprived of her rights under the Fifth Amendment of the Federal Constitution. The amendment says that no person can "be deprived of life, liberty, or property, without due process of law."

The case involved a 16-year-old Flushing High School senior who was accused of smuggling extensive notes into a Regents exam last January 25 on American History and World Backgrounds III.

After she had completed the examination, the student was taken to the office of the acting principal for questioning.

She first wrote out a statement denying that she had cheated; she said she had crammed until the last minute and had simply written down her notes quickly at the start of the three-hour exam, while the material was fresh in her mind, on the yellow scrap paper provided by the examination officials. The piece of paper containing her alleged "crib" notes was identical to the 6- by 9-inch scrap paper.

The acting principal refused to believe her and continued the interrogation for more than two hours more, during which the teen-ager reportedly became hysterical and finally signed a "confession" which read:

"I cheated." (Signature)

The acting principal, who was in charge of the high school because the principal was away on sabbatical leave,* told the story in these words in an affidavit* filed with the Supreme Court:

"Since it seemed impossible for the student to have written the notes, as she said she had, in a half-hour at the beginning of the examination, I challenged her, not to duplicate this feat, but just to copy over the notes as fast as she could on the same kind of 6 x 9

---

sabbatical leave—leave of absence.

affidavit—sworn statement.

paper. In twenty minutes, she had not succeeded in copying one quarter of her notes.

"I questioned the student again and she finally admitted to the cheating, whereupon I tore up her original statement and gave it back to her, asking her for a written statement of her new story. This she gave me. All through this she was in a highly excited, emotional state and in tears."

The next day, when she had calmed down, the student tried to retract her "confession." But the acting principal turned her down and, on January 31, he reported the alleged* cheating to the State Department of Education, the administrative arm of the Board of Regents.

The department then revoked all her Regents privileges. This meant that she was recorded as a cheater, given a zero on the test, and denied the right to take any future Regents examinations, including the Regents Scholarship and College Qualification Test, until her privileges were restored. It also meant that she was technically adjudged a criminal, since cheating on a Regents examination is a misdemeanor* under state law, although state officials yesterday could not recall any case ever prosecuted under this law.

The loss of Regents privileges prevents a student from receiving an academic diploma, which is almost always required for college admission. Instead, he receives a general or non-academic diploma.

Even if the privileges are reinstated, which is possible after a year if the student's behavior has been "exemplary" and if the high school principal recommends it, the black mark—the zero on the examination, signifying cheating—remains on his record. Many

---

alleged—suspected, but without proof.

misdemeanor—a minor crime.

colleges reject a student for this. After her loss of privileges, the student, who lives with her parents and a 15-year-old sister in Flushing, New York, went to the New York Civil Liberties Union on the advice of an uncle. Neil Fabricant, the organization's legislative director, took the case.

Mr. Fabricant first asked the city Board of Education for a hearing. The board agreed but said the attorney could only participate in the hearing as a passive observer. He refused this condition.

The board held the hearing anyway, but, according to Mr. Fabricant, did not inform him or the girl's family about it. The hearing officials concluded that the student had indeed cheated.

Shortly thereafter, Mr. Fabricant filed suit in the Supreme Court.

Justice Holtzman's decision said that the hearing was invalid because only the State Department of Education, and not the city department, was authorized to rule on such a case.

In addition, Judge Holtzman, although he made no legal ruling on whether or not the student had cheated or whether or not her "confession" was legally obtained, criticized the acting principal's interrogation methods. He indicated that in a criminal proceeding they would have been illegal.

Justice Holtzman still has to rule on what relief the student is entitled to. Because the question of whether or not she cheated has still not been resolved, she was graduated from Flushing High School last week with only a general diploma, leaving her college hopes in limbo.*

One possibility is that Mr. Holtzman will issue an

---

limbo—a state of uncertainty.

order requiring the State Department of Education to give her the impartial hearing with counsel that she was originally denied.

FURTHER INQUIRY

1. Do you agree or disagree with the position of (a) the student, (b) the principal, (c) the New York Civil Liberties Union? Explain your point of view.
2. Do you think that confessions obtained under pressure are legitimate in cases of (a) minor crimes, (b) major crimes?

This selection is one author's view of the legal aspects of wearing long hair in school. It is an issue which the American Civil Liberties Union has become increasingly concerned with as schools have sought to turn the fashion trend in boys' hair styles. In this article the author says that the choice of hair style is a form of self-expression and, as such, is protected by the First Amendment of the Constitution of the United States. Look up the amendment and see if you agree or disagree.

7. The Great Hair Problem

by SPENCER COXE

WHAT'S THE LAW SAY / Let's begin with the legal considerations, not necessarily the most important or fundamental aspect. Under our system of law, any government agency—including a school—is permitted to do only those things that are authorized by an Act of the Legislature. If the Legislature has not given the schools the powers to prescribe hair styles, the schools cannot do so, no matter how strongly a principal or teacher may feel. What do school laws say?

Of course, there are fifty different laws for fifty different states, and I have neither the space nor the knowledge to outline them all. But I believe that Pennsylvania is fairly typical. In Pennsylvania, the school law gives the school "the right to exercise the same

Spencer Coxe, "The Great Hair Problem," *Youth*, June 18, 1967. Reprinted by the American Civil Liberties Union, New York. Reprinted by permission of the American Civil Liberties Union.

Francis Pelletreau, a fifteen-year-old student at New Milford High School in New Jersey, was not permitted to attend classes because of his long hair. Girl students have faced similar problems with miniskirts and other "unconventional" attire (UPI)

authority as to conduct and behavior over the pupils attending school, . . . during the time they are in attendance, . . . as the parents . . . may exercise over them."

PARENTS CONTROL BEHAVIOR / According to ACLU's reading of this Pennsylvania statute, the school simply has no right to tell a child how he must have his hair cut, since hair style is neither "conduct" nor "behavior." Even assuming that length of hair is "behavior," the school, by prescribing hair style, is regulating the child's "behavior" while he is at home, since hair cannot be taken off at school and pasted back on at three o'clock. So the school is actually trying to assert a control over the child which is superior to the parents' control. The courts have held that the parents' control is superior to the school's.

To Maintain Discipline / School authorities have frequently claimed that they *must* outlaw weird styles in order to preserve discipline among the students. For instance, when 15-year-old David Harris was suspended from Haverford Junior High School, the Board upheld the suspension on the grounds that "the condition of the boy's hair obviously would tend to distract the attention of other students in the classroom and would tend to be a threat against reasonable discipline." The school authorities did not prove that David—who had a Prince Charles—*did* threaten discipline. They simply made a statement that something is "obvious" when it is not obvious at all. Is discipline really so shaky that the classroom is "threatened" and will go up in smoke if a kid comes in with a Prince Charles haircut? If so, why doesn't the teacher crack down on the kids that make the disturbance?

Too Much Made of Long Hair / The fact is, of course, that school authorities create the discipline problems themselves by making a great deal out of hair styles. There would be no problem if principals followed the example of Dr. Lewis Ashbee, Assistant Superintendent of high schools in San Francisco, who said, "Insofar as youngsters behave themselves and are clean, we ignore long hair and other juvenile aberrations* like mini-skirts." ACLU contends that the school's right to maintain discipline provides no legal basis for imposing standards of taste about hair style.

Who Is to Judge Acceptability / One reason that the hair controversy is important is that it has turned into a battleground between individuals and their government. When government tries to assert power that it does not possess, the situation is serious.

---

aberrations—departures from established systems and habits.

Even assuming that a state school law gives a school principal the power to prescribe hair styles, legal difficulties remain. Would such a law be constitutional? ACLU thinks not. In the first place, almost all the school regulations use such terms as "good grooming," "acceptable," and "extreme." Who is to say what these terms mean? "Acceptable" to whom? The very vagueness of these terms means that regulations based upon them are void. Such regulations depend upon totally subjective standards of taste.

RIGHT TO PRIVACY / Secondly and more important, governmental regulations about hair styles are an unconstitutional infringement upon the right of privacy and the right to be left alone, which Justice Brandeis* described as the most important right of all. These personal rights may not be curbed by a governmental body unless it can show some *compelling necessity*. In other words, the mere desire of a school principal —or, for that matter, the majority of the population and the Legislature—that school children look "neat" is no justification for *forcing* them to be neat on pain of suspension or expulsion. (By "compelling necessity" I refer to some such consideration as health and safety, which would certainly justify a principal's requiring that pupils' hair be louse-free or that girl students not wear highly inflammable dresses in cooking class.)

RIGHT TO SELF-EXPRESSION / The third and possibly most important constitutional argument against anti-hair regulations is that hair styles are a type of personal expression, and thus protected by the First Amendment. Many young people wear their hair the

---

Justice Brandeis—Justice Louis Dembitz Brandeis (1856–1941). He served as Associate Justice of the United States Supreme Court between 1916 and 1939 with great distinction.

way they do because it helps them to express their individuality. To many adults, such a form of expression may seem pretty foolish; still it is protected, along with other non-conformist expressions, by the Constitution. After all, adults are allowed to wear paper hats and make fools of themselves at New Year's Eve parties.

RESPECT FOR PARENTS / Our point has been that the law and the Constitution protect students from unwarranted interference by *government*. Constitutional rights, by and large, are rights protecting the individual against the *government,* not against other people. Juveniles are just as much protected in their rights to free expression, due process, and privacy as are adults. We have *not* said that juveniles have a constitutional or legal right to defy their parents.

LEGAL OPINIONS DIFFER / I have asserted rather positively that I believe that school regulations about hair styles are probably illegal and certainly unconstitutional. I should add that state court opinions are divided on the legal questions, and the United States Supreme Court has not yet ruled on the constitutional issues.

SHAPING THE FUTURE / When all is said and done, the great hair problem is not basically just a legal or constitutional issue. It raises even more important questions, namely, what kind of schools do we want and what kind of children do we want?

MINDS THAT QUESTION GROW / It seems to me that high school principals who fight with kids about their hair styles show that they are interested most in conformity and obedience. They conceive that the job of the school is to turn out little gentlemen who will "adjust" to what the school thinks is respectable society, i.e., society where men wear their hair short. It is also the job of the school, they think, to teach the young

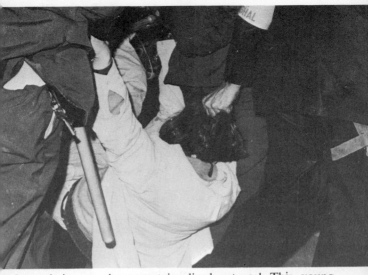

Long hair may have certain disadvantages! This young man is being removed from a demonstration (UPI)

to obey and show respect for authority, whether that authority is foolish or wise, right or wrong. I reject both of these views of education. I also reject the implied view that hair is important anyway. As columnist Russell Baker says, "Schools should be less concerned with unorthodox hair lengths and more concerned with why they are turning out so many orthodox minds."

EACH MAN IS UNIQUE / As for obedience, some school authorities, like the rest of the world, don't like to be told they are wrong, much less defied. It is the attitude of officialdom around the world. Once this kind of school principal takes a stand, he feels that he can't back down without losing face. So, right or wrong, he insists on inflicting his tastes about hair styles on the pupils, much as teachers a generation ago insisted on inflicting the flag salute on children whose religion taught them not to.

DEMOCRACY THRIVES ON LOYAL OPPOSITION / It is no accident that repressive societies have often sought to impose modes of dress and hair styles. The most recent example is mainland China where for years a national uniform has been foisted upon everybody and where more recently the Red Guards have been administering "pro-Peking" haircuts. The Red Chinese, like the Nazis before them, grasped the profound psychological truth that looking alike promotes thinking alike and acting alike.

In short, hair style has become an issue of symbolic importance. And symbols are important.

A NEVER-ENDING FIGHT / The refusal of high school youth to give in to the school over hair styles is part of the never-ending battle of the individual against statism. Again, the words of Justice Brandeis are applicable: "Experience should teach us to be most on our guard to protect liberty when the Government's purposes are beneficent. Men born to freedom are naturally alert to repel invasion of liberty by evil-minded rulers. The greatest dangers to liberty lurk in insidious encroachments by men of zeal, well-meaning, but without understanding."

FURTHER INQUIRY

1. In your view, does "long hair" interfere with learning? Does it contribute to disorder? Justify your position.
2. Do you regard hair style as behavior? Explain your position.
3. What is good grooming in terms of today's styles? Who should decide what good grooming is? Should teachers have a voice? Explain.

This selection appeared as an advertisement urging young men to resist the draft. It was published by an organization expressly established for the purpose of urging draft resistance. Does the right to a free press allow a newspaper to print such an ad? What justification, if any, exists for calling the fighting in Vietnam an illegal war? Are there ways of resisting other than those suggested here?

8. A Call to Resist Illegitimate Authority

by RESIST

To the Young Men of America, to the Whole of the American People, and to All Men of Good Will Everywhere:

1. An ever growing number of young American men are finding that the American war in Vietnam so outrages their deepest moral and religious sense that they cannot contribute to it in any way. We share their moral outrage.

Published by RESIST, Room 4, 763 Massachusetts Avenue, Cambridge, Massachusetts, 02139.

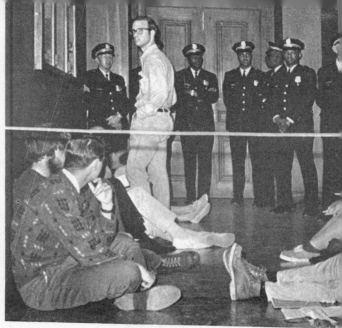

2. We further believe that the war is unconstitutional and illegal. Congress has not declared a war as required by the Constitution. Moreover, under the Constitution, treaties signed by the President and ratified by the Senate have the same force as the Constitution itself. The Charter of the United Nations is such a treaty. The Charter specifically obligates the United States to refrain from force or the threat of force in international relations. It requires member states to exhaust every peaceful means of settling disputes and to submit disputes which cannot be settled peacefully to the Security Council. The United States has systematically violated all of these Charter provisions for thirteen years.

3. Moreover, this war violates international agreements, treaties and principles of law which the United States Government has solemnly endorsed. The combat

These demonstrators are staging a sit-in at the Pentagon to protest the Vietnam war and the draft. There is much controversy about what means are legal and/or effective in protesting government policies (UPI)

role of the United States troops in Vietnam violates the Geneva Accord of 1954 which our government pledged to support but has since subverted. The destruction of rice, crops and livestock; the burning and bulldozing of entire villages consisting exclusively of civilian structures; the interning of civilian noncombatants in concentration camps; the summary executions of civilians in captured villages who could not produce satisfactory evidence of their loyalties or did not wish to be removed to concentration camps; the slaughter of peasants who dared to stand up in their fields and shake their fists at American helicopters—these are all actions of the kind which the United States and the other victorious powers of World War II declared to be crimes against humanity for which individuals were to be held personally responsible even when acting under the orders of their governments and for which Ger-

These people are defendants in a trial on charges that they conspired to help young men evade the draft. Among them are Dr. Benjamin Spock, William S. Coffin, Jr., and writer Mitchell Goodman (UPI)

mans were sentenced at Nuremberg to long prison terms and death. The prohibition of such acts as war crimes was incorporated in treaty law by the Geneva Conventions of 1949, ratified by the United States. These are commitments to other countries and to Mankind, and they would claim our allegiance even if Congress should declare war.

4. We also believe it is an unconstitutional denial of religious liberty and equal protection of the laws to withhold draft exemption from men whose religious

or profound philosophical beliefs are opposed to what in the Western religious tradition have been long known as unjust wars.

5. Therefore, we believe on all these grounds that every free man has a legal right and a moral duty to exert every effort to end this war, to avoid co!lusion* with it, and to encourage others to do the same. Young men in the armed forces or threatened with the draft

---

collusion—conspiring.

face the most excruciating choices. For them various forms of resistance risk separation from their families and their country, destruction of their careers, loss of their freedom and loss of their lives. Each must choose the course of resistance dictated by his conscience and circumstances. Among those already in the armed forces some are refusing to obey specific illegal and immoral orders, some are attempting to educate their fellow servicemen on the murderous and barbarous nature of the war, some are absenting themselves without official leave. Among those not in the armed forces some are applying for status as conscientious objectors to American aggression in Vietnam, some are refusing to be inducted. Among both groups some are resisting openly and paying a heavy penalty, some are organizing more resistance within the United States and some have sought sanctuary in other countries.

6. We believe that each of these forms of resistance against illegitimate authority is courageous and justified. Many of us believe that open resistance to the war and the draft is the course of action most likely to strengthen the moral resolve with which all of us can oppose the war and most likely to bring an end to the war.

7. We will continue to lend our support to those who undertake resistance to this war. We will raise funds to organize draft resistance unions, to supply legal defense and bail, to support families and otherwise aid resistance to the war in whatever ways may seem appropriate.

8. We firmly believe that our statement is the sort of speech that under the First Amendment must be free, and that the actions we will undertake are as legal as is the war resistance of the young men themselves. In any case, we feel that we cannot shrink from fulfilling our responsibilities to the youth whom many of us teach, to the country whose freedom we cherish, and to

the ancient traditions of religion and philosophy which we strive to preserve in this generation.

9. We call upon all men of good will to join us in this confrontation with immoral authority. Especially we call upon the universities to fulfill their mission of enlightenment and religious organizations to honor their heritage of brotherhood. *Now is the time to Resist.*

FURTHER INQUIRY

1. On what grounds could the people who drew up this paper be convicted of conspiring to counsel evasion of the draft? Would those who signed it also be guilty of conspiracy?
2. What is a war crime? Is is possible or likely that North Vietnam might also be guilty of war crimes? How can this be determined?
3. What is a conscientious objector? What alternative service is open to him?
4. Would you say that this statement is generally anti-war or only anti-Vietnam?

Civil disobedience may be defined as nonviolent resistance to a law. It is used to call attention to the fact that something in the law is wrong. But when should one resort to civil disobedience? Here, the author, Executive Director of the A. Philip Randolph Institute, suggests a number of questions which you may ask—and to which you must answer "yes"—before resorting to civil disobedience.

9. Civil Disobedience

by BAYARD RUSTIN

NUMBER 1: Are you attempting to break a law or are you attempting, rather, to adhere . . . to a higher principle in the hope that the law you break will be changed and that new law will emerge on the basis of that higher principle?

Number 2: Have you engaged in the democratic process and exercised the constitutional means that are available before engaging in the breaking of law?

From "Civil Disobedience, An Occasional Paper," by Bayard Rustin (Santa Barbara: The Center for the Study of Democratic Institutions, 1966), pp. 10–11. Reprinted by permission.

"We'll Defend You, Baby! Nobody's
Going to Push Our Gal Around!"

This cartoon implies that in an effort to gain freedom for themselves some people trample on the freedom of others who do not share their opinion (Courier-Journal, Louisville)

Number 3: Have you removed ego as much as it is possible to do so? That is to say, are you on this march because you want to get your picture in the paper, or because you are just mad at society, or because your mother doesn't want you to do this and you'll show her? Or are you here for impersonal, objective reasons?

Number 4: Do the people whom you ask to rebel feel there is a grievous wrong involved, and does your own rebellion help them to bring to the surface the inner feelings that they have but not previously have dared to express?

Number 5: Are you prepared cheerfully to accept the consequences of your acts? Through the civil rights struggle you yourself have fought against lying

Singer Joan Baez has served several prison terms for civil disobedience. She has been active in many antiwar demonstrations and deducts from her income tax the amount she feels goes toward the Vietnam war (UPI)

in the streets and being carried off by the police. When the policeman taps you on the shoulder and says, "You are under arrest," you believe you strengthen your ability to educate the people . . . who disagree with you by answering, "Yes, officer, I have broken the law because I believe it is wrong; I am perfectly willing to go with you. I do not want you to carry me." And when you get to the judge, you want to say to him, "I have done what society feels is wrong. I accept the punishment."

Number 6: Are you attempting to bring about a new social order by rebellion, or a new law that is better than the one that now exists?

The seventh and final question that one must ask

. . . Would the world be a better place if everybody, not just in your country and not just those who are black, but everyone in the world did likewise? Obviously, if everyone in the world were prepared to burn his draft card, war would not be possible.

FURTHER INQUIRY

1. Give examples of specific acts of civil disobedience in your community. Did such acts accomplish their purpose? Justify your answer.
2. What questions, if any, must one ask in order to test the desirability of taking part in civil disobedience?

In recent years there have been severe riots in many American cities, particularly in "black ghettos." The most infamous were the Detroit riot in the summer of 1967 and the Watts, Los Angeles, riot of 1965. However, there have been many in cities throughout the nation, including the Newark, New Jersey, riot of July, 1967. The following editorial comments on the causes of the riot. Consider: Do abused citizens have a right to riot? Can civil rights be gained in this way?

10. Riots in Our Cities— Newark and Beyond

by THE NEW YORK TIMES

THE sorry roll call of American cities ripped by summer riots grows. In Newark, National Guardsmen patrol the streets; in Hartford, a state of emergency has been declared; even in the heart of the nation's Corn Belt young Negroes riot in a small Iowa town.

The rioting is contagious, but it is not caused primarily by outside agitation. This is internal combustion.* The flame of frustration may be fanned by

---

internal combustion—fire begun without a match. Riots begun by and in communities without outsiders to start them. Outsiders are like matches. Matches are not needed to begin riots [fires].

militant cries of black power, but the combustible material is already present.

It is visible, but few whites experience it close up: the ratty conditions of slum dwellings; the slammed doors in the faces of job-seekers; the ghetto schools where learning is handicapped by inadequate faculties, facilities and funds; the countless humiliations in every-day existence for the poor who see the products—and the rewards—of American middle-class prosperity but can attain neither.

This scene shows the aftermath of the July, 1967, riots in Newark, New Jersey. The event that triggered the riot was the arrest of a cab driver (UPI)

Obviously none of this excuses the burning, looting and shooting. Lawbreaking must be prevented, order enforced and persons and property respected; but at the same time city officials and police officers must be aware that they are dealing almost entirely not with professional arsonists and thieves, but with flaming youth and burning adults living in summer tinder boxes.

In the name of their own self-interest as well as the rights of others, the rioters must be stopped. They must

109

be discouraged from violating the law. This cannot be successfully done with mere counter-violence.* A ghetto will not fit into a jailhouse. When men and women run amok* as they did in Newark yesterday, the force of civil authority must be exercised with firmness and with strength; and it must prevail. No one—Negro or white—must be left in any doubt about the futility as well as the criminality of such anarchic* violence as has now taken place in the streets of Newark.

The immediate aim has to be to restore calm in the troubled cities and to preserve it where no violence has broken out. There are many courses of action. Representatives of the strife-torn or the smoldering areas should be called together and their grievances heard. Members of the larger community and the so-called white establishment* certainly must participate. The Mayor and municipal leaders should "show the flag"—as some, including Mayor Lindsay, have already done—by personally getting out into the streets and entering houses instead of simply sending police cars when it is too late. Community relations groups should be formed where none exist. If there is no civilian police review board—and Newark has none—it ought to be created.

But all such measures, important as they may be to dampen down the tendency to riotous behavior, are only palliatives.* Cities will smolder until the walls

---

counter-violence—to answer violence with violence.

run amok—possessed with enough anger to kill.

anarchic—lawless.

white establishment—a term that refers to control of community force by the white group or segment.

palliatives—something which eases a situation but does not cure it.

that block Negro opportunity come tumbling down. Promises and even civil rights legislation alone will not do. The short fuse of frustrated Negroes will stop igniting only when the long-range, positive opportunities of modern American society are themselves brought nearer, and on a scale far greater than anything yet in sight. Anti-riot police will not prevent riots; pro-job, pro-education, pro-housing measures—in the long run—will.

FURTHER INQUIRY

1. Why have these riots occurred?
2. Why do nearly all of these riots begin with events involving the police?
3. Do you think that anti-riot police can prevent riots?
4. How do you believe that these riots can be prevented?
5. Do you think that people arrested during a riot are entitled to due process of law?

In 1896 the United States Supreme Court was called to rule upon separate but supposedly equal facilities for whites and Negroes on the railroads of Louisiana. In 1954, the Supreme Court was called upon to rule upon separate but supposedly equal facilities for whites and Negroes in the public schools of a number of states. *Plessy v. Ferguson* (1896) and *Brown v. Board of Education of Topeka* (1954) are classic illustrations of how the Supreme Court may change its mind.

Consider: Can separate facilities on railroads, in schools, or elsewhere ever be equal?

11. Separate but Equal: 1896-1954

SUPREME COURT OF THE UNITED STATES

A. *Plessy v. Ferguson:*

The object of the Fourteenth Amendment* was undoubtedly to enforce the absolute equality of the two races before the law, but in the nature of things it could not have been intended to abolish distinctions based upon color, or to enforce social as distinguished

---

Fourteenth Amendment—passed after the Civil War, amendment to extend the protection of the Bill of Rights to the states.

From *The United States Constitution in Perspective,* by Claude L. Heathcock (Boston: Allyn & Bacon, Inc., 1962), pp. 265–266, 288–290.

from political equality, or a co-mingling of the two races upon terms unsatisfactory to either. Laws permitting, and even requiring, their separation in places where they are liable to be brought into contact do not necessarily imply the inferiority of either race to the other, and have been generally, if not universally, recognized as within the competency* of the state legislatures in the exercise of their police power. The most common instance of this is connected with the establishment of separate schools for white and colored children,* which has been held to be a valid exercise of the legislative power even by courts of states where the political rights of the colored race have been longest and most earnestly enforced.

Laws forbidding intermarriage of the two races may be said in a technical sense to interfere with the freedom of contract, and yet have been universally recognized as within the police power of the state.

So far, then, as a conflict with the Fourteenth Amendment is concerned, the case reduces itself to the question whether the statute of Louisiana is reasonable regulation, and with respect to this there must necessarily be a large discretion on the part of the legislature. In determining the question of reasonableness it is at liberty to act with reference to the established usages, customs, and traditions of the people, and with a view to the promotion of their comfort, and the preservation of the public peace and good order. Gauged by this standard, we cannot say that a law which authorizes or even requires the separa-

---

competency—belonging to, in this instance, the powers of the state legislatures.

separate schools for white and colored children—here taken for granted and used as an argument for separate facilities elsewhere.

tion of two races in public conveyances is unreasonable, or more obnoxious to the Fourteenth Amendment than the acts of Congress requiring separate schools for colored children in the District of Columbia, the constitutionality of which does not seem to have been questioned, or the corresponding acts of state legislatures.

We consider the underlying fallacy of the plaintiff's argument to consist in the assumption that the enforced separation of the two races stamps the colored race with a badge of inferiority. If this be so, it is not by reason of anything found in the act, but solely because the colored race chooses to put that construction upon it. . . . The argument also assumes that social prejudices may be overcome by legislation, and that equal rights cannot be secured to the Negro except

Negroes stress the word "Now" in their grievances. As a people they were freed from slavery in 1865, but they argue that even after 100 years they are still accorded second-class citizenship (Robert Simmons)

by an enforced co-mingling of the two races. We cannot accept this proposition. If the two races are to meet on terms of social equality, it must be the result of natural affinities, a mutual appreciation of each other's merits and a voluntary consent of individuals.

B. *Brown v. Board of Education of Topeka:*

In the case of *Plessy v. Ferguson* . . . a three-judge federal district court denied relief to the plaintiff* on the so-called "separate but equal" doctrine. Under that doctrine, equality of treatment is accorded when races are provided substantially equal facilities, even though these facilities be separate.

---

relief to the plaintiff—a favorable decision for the person who brings in or starts legal action.

Does integrated schooling provide a better social as well as academic education for these children? Will they be more capable adult citizens in dealing with tomorrow's social problems? Will they be better able to live with their own people (Urban League)

The plaintiffs contend that segregated public schools are not "equal" and cannot be made "equal," and that hence they are deprived of the equal protection of the laws. . . .

In approaching this problem, we cannot turn the clock back to 1868 when this Amendment* was adopted, or even to 1896 when *Plessy v. Ferguson* was written. We must consider public education in the light of its full development and its present place in American life throughout the nation.

Today, education is perhaps the most important function of state and local government. Compulsory

1868 Amendment—Fourteenth Amendment.

school attendance laws and the great expenditure for education both demonstrate our recognition of the importance of education to our democratic society.

We come then to the question presented: Does segregation of children in public schools solely on the basis of race, even though the physical facilities and other "tangible" factors may be equal, deprive the children of the minority group of equal educational opportunity? We believe that it does.

Segregation of white and colored children in public schools has a detrimental effect upon the colored children. The impact is greater when it has the sanction of the law; for the policy of separating the races is usually interpreted as denoting the inferiority of the Negro group. A sense of inferiority affects the motivation of a child to learn.

We conclude that in the field of public education the doctrine of "separate but equal" has no place. Separate educational facilities are inherently unequal. Therefore, we hold that the plaintiffs and others similarly situated* for whom the actions have been brought are, by reason of the segregation complained

---

plaintiffs and others similarly situated—the only persons bound by this decision. Only the five school boards that were actually parties to the suit are bound by *Brown v. Board of Education of Topeka,* and the only laws held unconstitutional were those involved in the case. Generally, a rule of law handed down by the Court in a specific case will be accepted and complied with throughout the nation, but such compliance is technically voluntary since the Court's ruling can only apply to the parties involved in the case. This helps to explain why desegregation of school systems on a widespread basis has been slow—stubborn school boards can only be compelled to integrate their schools as cases are brought against them in the courts.

of, deprived of the equal protection of the laws guaranteed by the Fourteenth Amendment.

FURTHER INQUIRY

1. If separate facilities can indeed be equal in every way, should they be allowed to exist?
2. How can it be said that laws regulating marriage are within the police power of a state?
3. To what extent can laws overcome prejudice?
4. How is segregation damaging to school children?

In the fall of 1957, President Eisenhower used federal troops in order to force desegregation of Central High School in Little Rock, Arkansas. This event was a landmark in the struggle to implement the 1954 Brown decision. What follows is an interview conducted for NBC by a Norwegian correspondent, Mrs. Ricketts, with white and Negro students who were at Central High when the struggle took place. Sammy Dean Parker, Kay Baron, and Robin Woods were white girls who participated. Joseph Fox was a white boy and Ernest Green and Minnijean Brown were Negroes.

Consider: Why were some of the white students confused about their attitudes toward Negroes? How can young people help change the attitudes of their parents regarding integration?

12. Student Reactions to the Little Rock Affair of 1957

by ANTHONY LEWIS *and*
THE NEW YORK TIMES

MRS. RICKETTS: Do you think it is possible to start working this out on a more sensible basis than violent demonstration?

SAMMY: No, I don't because the South has always been against racial mixing and I think they will fight

From *Portrait of a Decade,* by Anthony Lewis and *The New York Times* (New York: Random House, Inc., 1962), pp. 63–66. Copyright © 1964 by The New York Times Company. Reprinted by permission of Random House, Inc.

In an attempt to integrate Central High School in Little Rock, Arkansas, Elizabeth Eckford is turned away by national guardsmen called out to prevent desegregation in defiance of a federal court order (UPI)

this thing to the end. . . . We fight for our freedom—
that's one thing. And we don't have any freedom any
more.

ERNEST: Sammy, you said that you don't have
freedom. I wonder what do you mean by it—that you
don't have freedom? You are guaranteed your freedoms in the Bill of Rights and your Constitution. You
have the freedom of speech—I noticed that has been
exercised a whole lot in Little Rock. The freedom of
petition, the freedom of religion and the other freedoms are guaranteed to you. As far as freedom, I
think that if anybody should kick about freedoms, it
should be us. Because I think we have been given a
pretty bad side on this thing as far as freedoms.

SAMMY: Do you call those troops freedom? I don't.
And I also do not call it free when you are being es-
corted into the school every morning.

ERNEST: You say why did the troops come here?
It is because our government—our state government—
went against the federal law. . . . Our country is set up
so that we have forty-eight states* and no one state
has the ability to overrule our nation's government. I
thought that was what our country was built around.
I mean, that is why we fight. We fought in World War
II together—the fellows that I know died in the Korean
War. I mean, why should my friends get out there and
die for a cause called "democracy" when I can't exercise my rights—tell me that.

ROBIN: I agree with Ernest.

JOE: Well, Sammy, I don't know what freedom has
been taken away from you because the truth is—I
know as a senior myself—the troops haven't kept me
from going to my classes or participating in any school
activity. I mean, they're there just to keep order in

---

forty-eight states—now we have fifty states.

case—I might use the term "hotheads"—get riled up. But I think as long as—if parents would just stay out of it and let the children of the school at Central High figure it out for themselves, I think it would be a whole lot better. I think the students are mature enough to figure it out for themselves. . . . As far as I'm concerned, I'll lay the whole blame of this trouble in Governor Faubus' lap.

SAMMY: I think we knew before this ever started that some day we were going to have to integrate the schools. And I think that our Governor was trying to protect all of us when he called out the National Guard—and he was trying to prepare us, I think.

ERNEST: . . . Well, I have to disagree. . . . I know a student that's over there with us, Elizabeth, and that young lady, she walked two blocks, I guess—as you all know—and the mob was behind her. Did the troops break up the mob?

The reality of integration in Little Rock's Hall High School may serve to counteract generations of racial prejudice which taught Negro inferiority. Here, Jacqueline F. Evans was the first Negro to be accepted in the school's National Honor Society (UPI)

ROBIN: . . . And when Elizabeth had to walk down in front of the school, I was there and I saw that. And may I say, I was very ashamed—I felt like crying—because she was so brave when she did that. And we just weren't behaving ourselves—just jeering her. I think if we had had any decency, we wouldn't have acted that way. But I think if everybody would just obey the Golden Rule—do unto others as you would have others do unto you—might be the solution. How would you like to have to . . . walk down the street with everybody yelling behind you like they yelled behind Elizabeth?

MRS. RICKETTS: Sammy, why do these children not want to go to school with Negroes?

SAMMY: Well, I think it is mostly race mixing.

MRS. RICKETTS: Race mixing? What do you mean?

SAMMY: Well, marrying each other.

MINNIJEAN: Hold your hand up. I'm brown; you

A fire bomb was tossed into this freedom rider bus by a local group against desegregation. Local police failed to investigate this group (Wide World)

are white. What's the difference? We are all of the same thoughts. You're thinking about your boy—he's going to the Navy. I'm thinking about mine—he's in the Air Force. We think about the same thing.

SAMMY: I'll have to agree with you.

ERNEST: Well, getting back to this intermarriage and all that. I don't know where people get all that. Why do I want to go to school? To marry with someone? I mean, school's not a marriage bureau. . . . I'm going there for an education, really. If I'm going there to socialize, I don't need to be going to school, I can stand out on the corner and socialize, as far as that.

MINNIJEAN: Kay, Joe and Robin—do you know anything about me, or is it just that your mother has told you about Negroes? . . .

MRS. RICKETTS: . . . Have you ever really made an effort to try to find out what they're like?

KAY: Not until today.

SAMMY: Not until today.

MRS. RICKETTS: And what do you think about it after today?

KAY: Well, you know that my parents and a lot of the other students and their parents think that the Negroes aren't equal to us. But—I don't know. It seems like they are, to me.

SAMMY: These people are—we'll have to admit that.

ERNEST: I think, like we're doing today, discussing our different views . . . if the people of Little Rock . . . would get together, I believe they would find out a different story—and try to discuss the thing instead of getting out in the street and kicking people around and calling names—and all that sort of thing. If . . . people got together it would be smoothed over.

KAY: I think that if our friends had been getting in this discussion today, I think that maybe some of them—not all of them—in time, they would change their mind. But probably some of them would change their mind today.

SAMMY: I know now that it isn't as bad as I thought it was—after we got together and discussed it.

KAY: [Sammy and I] We both came down here today with our minds set on it [that] we weren't going to change our mind that we were fully against integration. But I know now that we're going to change our minds.

MRS. RICKETTS: What do your parents say to that?

KAY: I think I'm going to have a long talk with my parents.

FURTHER INQUIRY

1. Why was it difficult for Minnijean Brown to attend Central High?
2. With which of the six students' remarks would you identify your own opinions? Why?
3. How would you imagine Kay's long talk with her parents after the program?
4. Why were some of the white students confused about their attitudes toward Negroes?
5. How can young people help change the attitudes of their parents regarding integration?

The struggle for civil rights and liberties has taken many forms. Not the least of these were the "freedom rides," the most notable of which began on May 4, 1961, in Washington, D.C., and ended on May 17, 1961, in New Orleans. Along the way the white and Negro riders tested segregated facilities in lunchrooms, waiting rooms, and on buses. By the end of the rides, many that had been at one time segregated were opened to white and black alike. What follows is a day-by-day account of one ride. Other freedom rides continued until November 1.

13. Freedom Ride Diary

by LOUIS E. LOMAX

May 4: Ride begins from Washington; arrives in Richmond.

May 7: Arrival in Danville (Va.); dispute over restaurant service settled quietly at Trailways terminal.

May 8: Arrival in Charlotte (N.C.); arrest of one rider for trespass while demanding shoeshine at Union bus terminal.

From *The Negro Revolt*, by Louis E. Lomax (New York: Signet paperback edition, 1962), pp. 147–156. Copyright © 1962 by Louis E. Lomax. Reprinted by permission of Harper & Row, Publishers.

May 9: Arrival in Rock Hill (S.C.) and attack in Greyhound terminal; white waiting room at Trailways terminal is closed when bus pulls in.

May 10: Defendant in Charlotte trespass case acquitted. Two riders arrested in Winnsboro (S.C.) and released after several hours; charges dropped.

May 12: Arrival in Augusta (Ga.); all facilities used.

May 13: Traveling through Athens (Ga.), where all facilities are used, and arrival in Atlanta; restaurant closed at Greyhound station. The Court of Appeals of the Fifth Circuit directs a lower court to "obliterate" the distinction between interstate and intrastate passengers at the train terminal in Birmingham. This is one of the many stations in the South with one waiting room for white and Negro interstate passengers and a second for Negro intrastate passengers.*

May 14: Some riders are served at Trailways terminal in Atlanta. Entire group leaves for Birmingham, riding in Trailways and Greyhound buses. Department of Justice advises Birmingham police it has received warnings of planned violence when buses reach their city. Greyhound bus met by mob in Anniston; passengers prevented from getting off. Tires slit and go flat six miles out of Anniston. Men following in automobiles attempt to board but are prevented by a state law enforcement officer who has been riding bus. An incendiary device thrown through a window sets fire to the bus; and it is completely destroyed. All passengers are removed, and 12 admitted to hospital, mostly for smoke inhalation; they later resume their ride to Birmingham. The Trailways bus also encounters the

---

intrastate passengers—within a state. Because Congress controls transportation between states, segregated facilities had been abolished for travelers journeying between states, but not for those traveling within a state.

(Magnum)

mob in Anniston and faced by it the driver orders
Negroes to the rear. One Negro and two white Riders
beaten. Bus continues on to Birmingham, where Riders
are attacked when they get off; one of them requires
over 50 stitches. At neither Anniston nor Birmingham
is anyone arrested. Despite warnings of probable trouble, no police are on hand at Birmingham, and none
arrive until ten minutes after fighting begins.

May 15: Greyhound bus drivers refuse to drive group on to Montgomery. Riders take plane for New Orleans, arriving there late at night. Governor Patterson issues his first statement, advising Riders to "get out of Alabama as quickly as possible."

Attorney General Kennedy* asks the state to provide police protection; the Governor first agrees, then changes his position.

May 16: Riders stay in seclusion in New Orleans. In Birmingham, three men are arrested for taking part in the attack of the 14th.

May 17: Riders meet at church in New Orleans and then disband. This ends the original CORE-planned ride.

FURTHER INQUIRY

1. In entering segregated facilities, the riders were breaking the law. To what extent, if any, is breaking the law justified?
2. How do you feel the failure of the police to be present on May 14th in Birmingham can be explained?
3. How do you account for the fact that whites participated in freedom rides designed to win rights for Negroes?
4. Why was the white terminal closed?

Attorney General Robert Kennedy—head of the Department of Justice. He was then elected senator from New York. Senator Kennedy was assassinated June 5, 1968, while campaigning for the presidential nomination of the Democratic party.

The following is a summary of the most important and far-reaching law passed in the area of civil rights. This law is referred to as the Civil Rights Act of 1964.

Consider: Why do you believe or disbelieve that carrying out this law will help give Negroes equal rights?

14. Summary of the Civil Rights Act of 1964

by THE NEW YORK TIMES

A DECADE after the Supreme Court decision which declared segregation in schools unconstitutional, the Congress passed, and President Lyndon B. Johnson signed, a sweeping civil rights bill. This new legislation wrote Negro equality into the nation's fundamental law. No longer simply the judgment of the courts, equal rights now became the will of Congress. Moreover,

"Summary of the Civil Rights Act of 1964," *The New York Times,* June 20, 1964, p. 10. Copyright © 1964 by The New York Times Company. Reprinted by permission.

every public opinion poll indicated that its provisions reflected the sense of the American people. Some historians called it the Negro's "Magna Carta."*

The Act covered nearly every aspect of public life. It guaranteed equal treatment not only in such matters as voting and publicly owned or operated facilities, but also employment and access to hotels, restaurants, gasoline stations and amusement areas. Of all the demands made by civil rights groups, only housing lay outside its jurisdiction. A mere recital of its main provisions conveys a quiet eloquence and represents in a unique way the redemption of a pledge made nearly two centuries ago in Philadelphia in the Declaration of Independence. A summary of its major provisions is presented here.

TITLE I. VOTING

Prohibits registrars* from applying different standards to white and Negro voting applicants because of inconsequential errors on their forms. Requires that literacy tests be in writing, except under special arrangements for blind persons, and that any applicant desiring one be given a copy of the questions and his answers. Makes a sixth-grade education a rebuttable presumption* of literacy.

Magna Carta—achievement of rights and liberties. In 1215 King John of England agreed to give certain Englishmen various rights incorporated in a document called Magna Carta.

registrars—election officials.

rebuttable presumption—assumes that a person with a sixth-grade education is literate.

TITLE II. PUBLIC ACCOMMODATION

Prohibits discrimination or refusal of service on account of race in hotels, motels, restaurants, gasoline stations and places of amusement if their operations affect interstate commerce or if their discrimination "is supported by state action." This permits the Attorney General to enforce the title by suit in the federal courts if he believes that any person or group is engaging in a "pattern or practice of resistance" to the rights declared by the title.

TITLE III. PUBLIC FACILITIES

Requires that Negroes have equal access to and treatment in publicly owned or operated facilities such as

132

The March on Washington, August 28, 1963, was a plea for greater civil rights legislation in education, voting, employment and the courts. The Civil Rights Act of 1964 closely defined and provided enforcement for the freedoms guaranteed every citizen in the Bill of Rights (Wide World)

parks, stadiums and swimming pools. Authorizes the Attorney General to sue for enforcement of these rights if private citizens are unable to sue effectively.

TITLE IV. PUBLIC SCHOOLS

Empowers the Attorney General to bring school desegregation suits under the same conditions as in Title III. Authorizes technical and financial aid to school districts to assist in desegregation.

TITLE V. CIVIL RIGHTS COMMISSION

Extends the life of the Civil Rights Commission until January 31, 1968.

In violation of local trespass laws, freedom riders, both black and white, integrated public lunch counters and waiting rooms in an unprecedented assertion of their right to equal services (Wide World)

TITLE VI. FEDERAL AID

Provides that no person shall be subjected to racial discrimination in any program receiving federal aid. Directs federal agencies to take steps against discrimination including—as a last resort, and after hearings —withholding of federal funds from state or local agencies that discriminate.

TITLE VII. EMPLOYMENT

Bans discrimination by employers or unions with one hundred or more employees or members the first year the Act is effective, reducing [the number] over four years to twenty-five or more. Establishes a commission to investigate alleged discrimination and use persuasion to end it. Authorizes the Attorney General to sue if he believes any person or group is engaged in a "pattern or practice" of resistance to the title, and to ask for trial by a three-judge court. . . .

TITLE VIII. STATISTICS

Directs the Census Bureau to compile statistics of registration and voting by race in areas of the country designated by the Civil Rights Commission. . . .

Limited job opportunities have long been an obstacle in the Negroes' drive for equality. Here demonstrators protest hiring practices in New York's building trades (CORE)

TITLE IX. COURTS

Permits appel!ate review* of decisions by federal district judges to send back to the state courts criminal defendants who have attempted to remove their cases on the ground that their civil rights would be denied in state trials.

TITLE X. CONCILIATION

Establishes a Community Relations Service in the Commerce Department to help conciliate* racial disputes. . . .

TITLE XI. MISCELLANEOUS

Guarantees jury trials for criminal contempt* under any part of the Act but Title I—a provision added in the Senate. Provides that the statute shall not invalidate state laws with consistent purposes,* and that it shall not impair any existing powers of federal officials.

---

appellate review—a court that would hear appeals.

conciliate—settle.

criminal contempt—disregard of or refusal to comply with court order.

statute shall not invalidate state laws with consistent purposes—shall not interfere with the right of the state to enforce similar laws passed by its own legislature.

FURTHER INQUIRY

1. How do each of the twelve titles of this law help us to understand some of the problems of civil rights?
2. Why is it important that the Attorney General and the Justice Department may participate in court action to promote civil rights?
3. Why do you believe or disbelieve that the enforcement of this law will help give Negroes equal rights?
4. Why do you think that Title II: Public Accommodation is the most controversial section of the law?

The following reading comes from the United Nation's *Universal Declaration of Human Rights,* adopted in Paris, 1948, by the United Nations General Assembly. The declaration contains thirty articles of which ten are included here.

The problems of civil liberties and civil rights are international in scope. The following document attempts to put down in writing a code that would apply to people throughout the world. Why do you believe a document such as this was written? How would you compare this statement with the first ten amendments to the United States Constitution (Bill of Rights)? How do you believe the ideals of this Declaration may be brought about in the future?

15. The Universal Declaration of Human Rights

by THE UNITED NATIONS

ARTICLE 1. All human beings are born free and equal in dignity and rights. They are endowed with reason and conscience and should act towards one another in a spirit of brotherhood.

ARTICLE 2. Everyone is entitled to all the rights and freedoms set forth in this Dec'aration, without distinction of any kind, such as race, color, sex, lan-

From "The Universal Declaration of Human Rights," UNESCO *Courier,* Dec., 1963, pp. 16–17.

In 1965 in the South, Negroes tried by demonstration to get the rights promised to them by law. In Selma, Alabama, where this picture was taken, civil rights workers attempted a peaceful march and were forcibly disbanded by police (Black Star)

guage, religion, political or other opinion, national or social origin, property, birth or other status. . . .

ARTICLE 3. Everyone has the right to life, liberty and security of person.

ARTICLE 4. No one shall be held in slavery or servitude; slavery and the slave trade shall be prohibited in all their forms.

ARTICLE 5. No one shall be subjected to torture or to cruel, inhuman or degrading treatment or punishment.

ARTICLE 6. Everyone has the right to recognition everywhere as a person before the law.

ARTICLE 7. All are equal before the law and are entitled without any discrimination to equal protection of the law. All are entit'ed to equal protection against any discrimination in violation of this Declaration and against any incitement to such discrimination.

ARTICLE 8. Everyone has the right to an effective remedy by the competent national tribunals* for acts violating the fundamental rights granted him by the constitution or by law.

ARTICLE 9. No one shall be subjected to arbitrary arrest,* detention,* or exile.

ARTICLE 10. Everyone is entitled in full equality to a fair and public hearing by an independent and impartial tribunal* in the determination of his rights and obligations and of any criminal charge against him.

---

competent national tribunals—rightful courts.

arbitrary arrest—arrest without lawful procedure.

detention—held in jail.

impartial tribunal—a just court which hears all sides and decides fairly.

FURTHER INQUIRY

1. Why do you believe or not believe that our nation should ratify this Declaration?
2. Why would it be difficult for the provisions of this Declaration to be enforced?
3. How are human rights related to civil rights and liberties?

Part Three

Appendix

THE CONSTITUTION OF THE
UNITED STATES

Adopted September 17, 1787
Effective March 4, 1789

We the People of the United States, in order to form a more perfect Union, establish Justice, ensure domestic Tranquillity, provide for the common defence, promote the general Welfare, and secure the Blessings of Liberty to ourselves and our Posterity, do ordain and establish this Constitution for the United States of America.

ARTICLE I

Section 1. All legislative powers herein granted shall be vested in a Congress of the United States, which shall consist of a Senate and House of Representatives.

Section 2. The House of Representatives shall be composed of members chosen every second year by the people of the several states, and the electors in each state shall have the qualifications requisite for electors of the most numerous branch of the state legislature.

No person shall be a representative who shall not have attained to the age of twenty-five years, and been seven years a citizen of the United States, and who shall not, when elected, be an inhabitant of that state in which he shall be chosen.

Representatives and direct taxes shall be apportioned among the several states which may be included within this union, according to their respective numbers, which shall be determined by adding to the whole number of free persons, including those bound to service for a term of years, and excluding Indians not taxed, three-fifths of all other persons. The actual enumeration shall be made within three years after the first meeting of the Congress of the United States, and within every subsequent term of ten years, in such manner as they shall by law direct. The number of representatives shall not exceed one for every 30,000, but each state shall have at least one representative; and until such enumeration shall be made, the state of New Hampshire shall be entitled to choose three, Massachusetts eight, Rhode Island and Providence Plantations one, Connecticut five, New York six, New Jersey four, Pennsylvania eight, Delaware one, Maryland six, Virginia ten, North Carolina five, South Carolina five, and Georgia three.

When vacancies happen in the representation from any state, the executive authority thereof shall issue writs of election to fill such vacancies.

The House of Representatives shall choose their speaker and other officers; and shall have the sole power of impeachment.

Section 3. The Senate of the United States shall be composed of two senators from each state, chosen by the legislature thereof, for six years, and each senator shall have one vote.

Immediately after they shall be assembled in consequence of the first election, they shall be divided as equally as may be into three classes. The seats of the senators of the first class shall be vacated at the expiration of the second year, of the second class at the expiration of the fourth year, and of the third class at the expiration of the sixth year, so that one-third may be chosen every second year; and if vacancies happen by resignation, or otherwise, during the recess of the legislature of any state, the executive thereof may make temporary appointments until the next meeting of the legislature, which shall then fill such vacancies.

No person shall be a senator who shall not have attained to the age of 30 years, and been nine years a citizen of the United States, and who shall not, when elected, be an inhabitant of that state for which he shall be chosen.

The Vice-President of the United States shall be president of the Senate, but shall have no vote, unless they be equally divided.

The Senate shall choose their other officers, and also a president *pro tempore,* in the absence of the Vice-President, or when he shall exercise the office of President of the United States.

The Senate shall have the sole power to try all impeachments. When sitting for that purpose, they shall be on oath or affirmation. When the President of the United States is tried, the chief justice shall preside: And no person shall be convicted without the concurrence of two-thirds of the members present.

Judgment in cases of impeachment shall not extend further than to removal from office, and disqualification to hold and enjoy any office of honor, trust or profit under the United States; but the party convicted shall nevertheless be liable and subject to indictment, trial, judgment and punishment, according to law.

Section 4. The times, places and manner of holding elections for senators and representatives, shall be prescribed in each state by the legislature thereof: but the Congress may at any time by law make or alter such regulations, except as to the places of choosing senators.

The Congress shall assemble at least once in every year, and such meeting shall be on the first Monday in December, unless they shall by law appoint a different day.

Section 5. Each house shall be the judge of the elections, returns and qualifications of its own members, and a majority of each shall constitute a quorum to do business; but a smaller number may adjourn from day to day, and may be authorized to compel the attendance of absent members, in such manner, and under such penalties as each house may provide.

Each house may determine the rules of its proceedings, punish its members for disorderly behavior, and, with the concurrence of two-thirds, expel a member.

Each house shall keep a journal of its proceedings, and from time to time publish the same, excepting such parts as may, in their judgment, require secrecy; and the yeas and nays of the members of either house on any question shall, at the desire of one-fifth of those present, be entered on the journal.

Neither house, during the session of Congress, shall, without the consent of the other, adjourn for more than three days, nor to any other place than that in which the two houses shall be sitting.

Section 6. The senators and representatives shall receive a compensation for their services, to be ascertained by law, and paid out of the Treasury of the United States. They shall in all cases, except treason, felony and breach of the peace, be privileged from arrest during their attendance at the session of their respective houses, and in going to and returning from the same; and for any speech or debate in either house, they shall not be questioned in any other place.

No senator or representative shall, during the time for which he was elected, be appointed to any civil office under the authority of the United States, which shall have been created, or the emoluments whereof shall have been increased during such time; and no person holding any office under the United States, shall be a member of either house during his continuance in office.

Section 7. All bills for raising revenue shall originate in the House of Representatives; but the Senate may propose or concur with amendments as on other bills.

Every bill which shall have passed the House of Representatives and the Senate, shall, before it become a law, be presented to the President of the United States; if he approve, he shall sign it, but if not, he shall return it, with his objections, to that house in which it shall have originated, who shall enter the objections at large on their journal, and proceed to reconsider it. If after such reconsideration, two-thirds of that house shall agree to pass the bill, it shall be sent, together with the objections, to the other house, by which it shall likewise be reconsidered, and if approved by two-thirds of that house, it shall become a law. But in all such cases the votes of both houses shall be determined by yeas and nays, and the names of the persons voting for and against the bill shall be entered on the journal of each house respectively. If any bill shall not be returned by the President within ten days (Sundays excepted), after it shall have been presented to him, the same shall be a law, in like manner as if he had signed it, unless the Congress by their adjournment prevent its return, in which case it shall not be a law.

Every order, resolution, or vote to which the concurrence of the Senate and House of Representatives may be necessary (except on a question of adjournment), shall be presented to the President of the United States; and before the same shall take effect, shall be approved by him, or, being disapproved by him, shall be re-passed by two-thirds of the Senate and House of Representatives, according to the rules and limitations prescribed in the case of a bill.

Section 8. The Congress shall have power:

To lay and collect taxes, duties, imposts and excises, to pay the debts and provide for the common defence and general welfare of the United States; but all duties, imposts and excises shall be uniform throughout the United States:

To borrow money on the credit of the United States:

To regulate commerce with foreign nations, and among the several states, and with the Indian tribes:

To establish an uniform rule of naturalization, and uniform laws on the subject of bankruptcies throughout the United States:

To coin money, regulate the value thereof, and of foreign coin, and fix the standard of weights and measures:

To provide for the punishment of counterfeiting the securities and current coin of the United States:

To establish post-offices and post-roads:

To promote the progress of science and useful arts, by securing for limited times to authors and inventors the exclusive right to their respective writings and discoveries:

To constitute tribunals inferior to the Supreme Court:

To define and punish piracies and felonies committed on the high seas, and offences against the law of nations:

To declare war, grant letters of marque and reprisal, and make rules concerning captures on land and water:

To raise and support armies, but no appropriation of money to that use shall be for a longer term than two years:

To provide and maintain a navy:

To make rules for the government and regulation of the land and naval forces:

To provide for calling forth the militia to execute the laws of the Union, suppress insurrections and repel invasions:

To provide for organizing, arming and disciplining the militia, and for governing such part of them as may be employed in the service of the United States, reserving to the states respectively, the appointment of the officers, and the authority of training the militia according to the discipline prescribed by Congress:

To exercise exclusive legislation in all cases whatsoever, over such district (not exceeding ten miles square) as may, by cession of particular states, and the acceptance of Congress, become the seat of the government of the United States, and to exercise like authority over all places purchased by the consent of the legislature of the state in which the same shall be, for the erection of forts, magazines, arsenals, dockyards, and other needful buildings: and,

To make all laws which shall be necessary and proper for carrying into execution the foregoing powers, and all other powers vested by this Constitution in the government of the United States, or in any department or officer thereof.

Section 9. The migration or importation of such persons as any of the states now existing shall think proper to admit, shall not be prohibited by the Congress prior to the year 1808, but a tax or duty may be imposed on such importations, not exceeding ten dollars for each person.

The privilege of the writ of *habeas corpus* shall not be suspended, unless when in cases of rebellion or invasion the public safety may require it.

No bill of attainder or *ex post facto* law shall be passed.

No capitation, or other direct tax shall be laid unless in proportion to the *census* or enumeration herein before directed to be taken.

No tax or duty shall be laid on articles exported from any state.

No preference shall be given by any regulation of commerce or revenue to the ports of one state over those of another: nor shall vessels bound to, or from one state, be obliged to enter, clear, or pay duties in another.

No money shall be drawn from the Treasury but in consequence of appropriations made by law; and a regular statement and account of the receipts and expenditures of all public money shall be published from time to time.

No title of nobility shall be granted by the United States: and no person holding any office of profit or trust under them, shall, without the consent of the Congress, accept of any present, emolument, office, or title, of any kind whatever, from any king, prince or foreign state.

Section 10. No state shall enter into any treaty, alliance, or confederation; grant letters of marque and reprisal; coin money; emit bills of credit; make any thing but gold and silver coin a tender in payment of debts; pass any bill of attainder, *ex post facto* law, or law impairing the obligation of contracts, or grant any title of nobility.

No state shall, without the consent of the Congress, lay any imposts or duties on imports or exports, except what may be absolutely necessary for executing its inspection laws; and the net produce of all duties and imposts, laid by any state on imports and exports, shall be for the use of the Treasury of the United States; and all such laws shall be subject to the revision and control of the Congress.

No state shall, without the consent of Congress, lay any duty of tonnage, keep troops, or ships of war in time of peace, enter into any agreement or compact with another state, or with a foreign power, or engage in war, unless actually invaded, or in such imminent danger as will not admit of delay.

ARTICLE II

Section 1. The executive power shall be vested in a President of the United States of America. He shall hold his office during the term of four years, and, together with the Vice-President, chosen for the same term, be elected as follows:

Each state shall appoint, in such manner as the legislature thereof may direct, a number of electors, equal to the whole number of senators and representatives to which the state may be entitled in the

Congress; but no senator or representative, or person holding an office of trust or profit under the United States, shall be appointed an elector.

The electors shall meet in their respective states, and vote by ballot for two persons, of whom one at least shall not be an inhabitant of the same state with themselves. And they shall make a list of all the persons voted for, and of the number of votes for each; which list they shall sign and certify, and transmit sealed to the seat of the government of the United States, directed to the president of the Senate. The president of the Senate shall, in the presence of the Senate and House of Representatives, open all the certificates and the votes shall then be counted. The person having the greatest number of votes shall be the President, if such number be a majority of the whole number of electors appointed; and if there be more than one who have such majority, and have an equal number of votes, then the House of Representatives shall immediately choose by ballot one of them for President; and if no person have a majority, then from the five highest on the list, the said House shall, in like manner, choose the President. But in choosing the President, the votes shall be taken by states, the representation from each state having one vote; a quorum for this purpose shall consist of a member or members from two-thirds of the states, and a majority of all the states shall be necessary to a choice. In every case, after the choice of the President, the person having the greatest number of votes of the electors shall be the Vice-President. But if there should remain two or more who have equal votes, the Senate shall choose from them by ballot the Vice-President.

The Congress may determine the time of choosing the electors, and the day on which they shall give their votes; which day shall be the same throughout the United States.

No person except a natural born citizen, or a citizen of the United States, at the time of the adoption of this constitution, shall be eligible to the office of President; neither shall any person be eligible to that office, who shall not have attained to the age of thirty-five years, and been fourteen years a resident within the United States.

In case of the removal of the President from office, or of his death, resignation, or inability to discharge the powers and duties of the said office, the same shall devolve on the Vice-President, and the Congress may by law provide for the case of removal, death, resignation, or inability, both of the President and Vice-President, declaring what officer shall then act as President, and such officer shall act accordingly, until the disability be removed, or a President shall be elected.

The President shall, at stated times, receive for his services, a compensation, which shall neither be increased nor diminished during the period for which he shall have been elected, and he shall not receive within that period any other emolument from the United States, or any of them.

Before he enter on the execution of his office, he shall take the following oath or affirmation:

"I do solemnly swear (or affirm) that I will faithfully execute the office of President of the United States, and will to the best of my ability, preserve, protect and defend the Constitution of the United States."

Section 2. The President shall be commander-in-chief of the army and navy of the United States, and of the militia of the several states, when called into the actual service of the United States; he may require the opinion, in writing, of the principal officer in each of the executive departments, upon any subject relating to the duties of their respective offices, and he shall have power to grant reprieves and pardons for offences against the United States, except in cases of impeachment.

He shall have power, by and with the advice and consent of the Senate, to make treaties, provided two-thirds of the senators present concur; and he shall nominate, and by and with the advice and consent of the Senate, shall appoint ambassadors, other public ministers and consuls, judges of the Supreme Court, and all other officers of the United States, whose appointments are not herein otherwise provided for, and which shall be established by law. But the Congress may by law vest the appointment of such inferior officers, as they think proper in the President alone, in the courts of law, or in the heads of departments.

The President shall have power to fill up all vacancies that may happen during the recess of the Senate, by granting commissions, which shall expire at the end of their next session.

Section 3. He shall, from time to time, give to the Congress information of the state of the Union, and recommend to their consideration, such measures as he shall judge necessary and expedient; he may, on extraordinary occasions, convene both houses, or either of them, and in case of disagreement between them, with respect to the time of adjournment, he may adjourn them to such time as he shall think proper; he shall receive ambassadors and other public ministers; he shall take care that the laws be faithfully executed, and shall commission all the officers of the United States.

Section 4. The President, Vice-President, and all civil officers of the United States shall be removed from office on impeachment for, and conviction of, treason, bribery, or other high crimes and misdemeanors.

ARTICLE III

Section 1. The judicial power of the United States, shall be vested in one Supreme Court, and in such inferior courts as the Congress may, from time to time, ordain and establish. The judges, both of the Supreme and inferior courts, shall hold their offices during good behavior, and shall, at stated times, receive for their services a compensation, which shall not be diminished during their continuance in office.

Section 2. The judicial power shall extend to all cases, in law and equity, arising under this Constitution, the laws of the United States, and treaties made, or which shall be made under their authority; to all cases affecting ambassadors, other public ministers and consuls; to all cases of admiralty and maritime jurisdiction; to controversies to which the United States shall be a party: to controversies between two or more states, between a state and citizens of another state, between citizens of different states, between citizens of the same state, claiming lands under grants of different states, and between a state, or the citizens thereof, and foreign states, citizens or subjects.

In all cases affecting ambassadors, other public ministers and consuls, and those in which a state shall be party, the Supreme Court shall have original jurisdiction. In all the other cases before-mentioned, the Supreme Court shall have appellate jurisdiction, both as to law and fact, with such exceptions, and under such regulations as the Congress shall make.

The trial of all crimes, except in cases of impeachment, shall be by jury; and such trial shall be held in the state where the said crimes shall have been committed; but when not committed within any state, the trial shall be at such place or places as the Congress may by law have directed.

Section 3. Treason against the United States shall consist only in levying war against them, or in adhering to their enemies, giving them aid and comfort. No person shall be convicted of treason unless on the testimony of two witnesses to the same overt act, or on confession in open court.

The Congress shall have power to declare the punishment of treason, but no attainder of treason shall work corruption of blood, or forfeiture, except during the life of the person attainted.

ARTICLE IV

Section 1. Full faith and credit shall be given in each state to the public acts, records and judicial proceedings of every other state. And the Congress may by general laws prescribe the manner in which such acts, records and proceedings shall be proved, and the effect thereof.

Section 2. The citizens of each state shall be entitled to all privileges and immunities of citizens in the several states.

A person charged in any state with treason, felony, or other crime, who shall flee from justice, and be found in another state, shall, on demand of the executive authority of the state from which he fled, be delivered up, to be removed to the state having jurisdiction of the crime.

No person held to service or labor in one state, under the laws thereof, escaping into another, shall, in consequence of any law or regulation therein, be discharged from such service or labor, but shall be delivered up on claim of the party to whom such service or labor may be due.

Section 3. New states may be admitted by the Congress into this Union; but no new state shall be formed or erected within the jurisdiction of any other state, nor any state be formed by the junction of two or more states, or parts of states, without the consent of the legislatures of the states concerned, as well as of the Congress.

The Congress shall have power to dispose of and make all needful rules and regulations respecting the territory or other property belonging to the United States; and nothing in this Constitution shall be so construed as to prejudice any claims of the United States, or of any particular state.

Section 4. The United States shall guarantee to every state in this Union, a republican form of government, and shall protect each of them against invasion; and on application of the legislature, or of the executive (when the legislature cannot be convened), against domestic violence.

ARTICLE V

The Congress, whenever two-thirds of both houses shall deem it necessary, shall propose amendments to this Constitution, or on the application of the legislatures of two-thirds of the several states, shall call a convention for proposing amendments, which, in either case, shall be valid to all intents and purposes, as part of this Constitution, when ratified by the legislatures of three-fourths of the several states, or by conventions in three-fourths thereof, as the one or the other mode of ratification may be proposed by the Congress: Provided, that no amendment which may be made prior to the year 1808, shall in any manner affect the first and fourth clauses in the ninth section of the first article; and that no state, without its consent, shall be deprived of its equal suffrage in the Senate.

ARTICLE VI

All debts contracted and engagements entered into, before the adoption of this Constitution, shall be as valid against the United States under this Constitution, as under the Confederation.

This Constitution, and the laws of the United States which shall be made in pursuance thereof; and all treaties made, or which shall be made, under the authority of the United States, shall be the supreme law of the land; and the judges in every state shall be bound thereby, any thing in the constitution or laws of any state to the contrary notwithstanding.

The senators and representatives before-mentioned, and the members of the several state legislatures, and all executive and judicial officers, both of the United States and of the several states, shall be bound by oath or affirmation, to support this Constitution; but no 'religious test shall ever be required as a qualification to any office or public trust under the United States.

ARTICLE VII

The ratification of the conventions of nine states, shall be sufficient for the establishment of this Constitution between the states so ratifying the same.

Done in convention, by the unanimous consent of the states present, the 17th day of September, in the year of our Lord 1787, and of the independence of the United States of America the 12th. In witness whereof we have hereunto subscribed our names.

George Washington, President, and Deputy from Virginia.

New Hampshire	John Langdon, Nicholas Gilman.
Massachusetts	Nathaniel Gorham, Rufus King.
Connecticut	William Samuel Johnson, Roger Sherman.
New York	Alexander Hamilton.
New Jersey	William Livingston, David Brearly, William Paterson, Jonathan Dayton.

Pennsylvania	Benjamin Franklin, Thomas Mifflin, Robert Morris, George Clymer, Thomas Fitzsimmons, Jared Ingersoll, James Wilson, Gouverneur Morris.
Delaware	George Read, Gunning Bedford, jun., John Dickinson, Richard Bassett, Jacob Broom.
Maryland	James McHenry, Daniel of St. Thomas Jenifer, Daniel Carroll.
Virginia	John Blair, James Madison, jun.
North Carolina	William Blount, Richard Dodds Spaight, Hugh Williamson.
South Carolina	John Rutledge, Charles Cotesworth Pinckney, Charles Pinckney, Pierce Butler.
Georgia	William Few, Abraham Baldwin.

Attest: William Jackson, Secretary.

AMENDMENTS TO THE CONSTITUTION

ARTICLE I

Congress shall make no law respecting an establishment of religion, or prohibiting the free exercise thereof; or abridging the freedom of speech or of the press; or the right of the people peaceably to assemble, and to petition the government for a redress of grievances.

ARTICLE II

A well-regulated militia being necessary to the security of a free state, the right of the people to keep and bear arms shall not be infringed.

ARTICLE III

No soldier shall, in time of peace, be quartered in any house without the consent of the owner, nor in time of war but in a manner to be prescribed by law.

ARTICLE IV

The right of the people to be secure in their persons, houses, papers, and effects, against unreasonable searches and seizures, shall not be violated, and no warrants shall issue but upon probable cause, supported by oath or affirmation, and particularly describing the place to be searched, and the persons or things to be seized.

ARTICLE V

No person shall be held to answer for a capital or otherwise infamous crime unless on a presentment or indictment of a grand jury, except in cases arising in the land or naval forces, or in the militia, when in actual service, in time of war or public danger; nor shall any person be subject for the same offence to be twice put in jeopardy of life or limb; nor shall be compelled in any criminal case to be a witness against himself, nor be deprived of life, liberty, or property, without due process of law; nor shall private property be taken for public use without just compensation.

ARTICLE VI

In all criminal prosecutions, the accused shall enjoy the right to a speedy and public trial, by an impartial jury of the state and district wherein the crime shall have been committed, which district shall have been previously ascertained by law, and to be informed of the nature and cause of the accusation; to be confronted with the witnesses against him; to have compulsory process for obtaining witnesses in his favor, and to have the assistance of counsel for his defense.

ARTICLE VII

In suits at common law, where the value in controversy shall exceed twenty dollars, the right of trial by jury shall be preserved, and no fact tried by a jury shall be otherwise re-examined in any court of the United States than according to the rules of the common law.

ARTICLE VIII

Excessive bail shall not be required, nor excessive fines imposed, nor cruel and unusual punishments inflicted.

ARTICLE IX

The enumeration in the Constitution of certain rights shall not be construed to deny or disparage others retained by the people.

ARTICLE X

The powers not delegated to the United States by the Constitution, nor prohibited by it to the states, are reserved to the states respectively, or to the people.

[The foregoing ten amendments were adopted at the first session of Congress, and were declared to be in force, December 15, 1791.]

ARTICLE XI

The judicial power of the United States shall not be construed to extend to any suit in law or equity, commenced or prosecuted against one of the United States, by citizens of another state, or by citizens or subjects of any foreign state.

[Declared in force, January 8, 1798.]

ARTICLE XII

The electors shall meet in their respective states, and vote by ballot for President and Vice-President, one of whom at least shall not be an inhabitant of the same state with themselves; they shall name in their ballots the person voted for as President, and in distinct ballots the person voted for as Vice-President; and they shall make distinct lists of all persons voted for as President, and of all persons voted for as Vice-President, and of the number of votes for each, which lists they shall sign and certify, and transmit, sealed, to the seat of the government of the United States directed to the president of the Senate; the president of the Senate shall, in the presence of the Senate and House of Representatives, open all the certificates, and the votes shall then be counted; the person having the greatest number of votes for President shall be the President, if such number be a majority of the whole number of electors appointed; and if no person have such majority, then from the persons having the highest numbers not exceeding three, on the list of those voted for as President, the House of Representatives shall choose immediately, by ballot, the President. But in choosing the President, the votes shall be taken by states, the representation from each state having one vote; a quorum for this purpose shall consist of a member or members from two-thirds of the states, and a majority of all the states shall be necessary to a choice. And if the House of Representatives shall not choose a President, whenever the right of choice shall devolve upon them, before the fourth day of March next following, then the Vice-President shall act as President, as in the case of the death or other constitutional disability of the President. The person having the greatest number of votes as Vice-President shall be the Vice-President, if such number be a majority of the whole number of electors appointed, and if no person have a majority, then from the two highest numbers on the list the Senate shall choose the Vice-President; a quorum for the purpose shall consist of two-thirds of the whole number of senators, and a majority of the whole number shall be necessary to a choice. But no person constitutionally ineligible to the office of President shall be eligible to that of Vice-President of the United States.

[Declared in force, September 25, 1804.]

ARTICLE XIII

Section 1. Neither slavery nor involuntary servitude, except as a punishment for crime whereof the party shall have been duly convicted, shall exist within the United States, or any place subject to their jurisdiction.

Section 2. Congress shall have power to enforce this article by appropriate legislation.

[Declared in force, December 18, 1865.]

ARTICLE XIV

Section 1. All persons born or naturalized in the United States, and subject to the jurisdiction thereof, are citizens of the United States and of the state wherein they reside. No state shall make or enforce any law which shall abridge the privileges or immunities of citizens of the United States; nor shall any state deprive any person of life, liberty, or property without due process of law; nor deny to any person within its jurisdiction the equal protection of the laws.

Section 2. Representatives shall be apportioned among the several states according to their respective numbers, counting the whole number of persons in each state, excluding Indians not taxed. But when the right to vote at any election for the choice of electors for President and Vice-President of the United States, representatives in Congress, the executive and judicial officers of a state, or the members of the legislature thereof, is denied to any of the male members of such state being of twenty-one years of age, and citizens of the United States or in any way abridged, except for participation in rebellion or other crime, the basis of representation therein shall be reduced in the proportion which the number of such male citizens shall bear to the whole number of male citizens twenty-one years of age in such state.

Section 3. No person shall be a senator or representative in Congress, or elector of President and Vice-President, or hold any office, civil or military, under the United States, or under any state, who, having previously taken an oath, as a member of Congress, or as an officer of the United States, or as a member of any state legislature, or as an executive or judicial officer of any state, to support the Constitution of the United States, shall have engaged in insurrection or rebellion against the same, or given aid and comfort to the enemies thereof. But Congress may, by a vote of two-thirds of each House, remove such disability.

Section 4. The validity of the public debt of the United States, authorized by law, including debts incurred for payment of pensions and bounties for services in suppressing insurrection or rebellion, shall not be questioned. But neither the United States nor any state shall assume or pay any debt or obligation incurred in aid of insurrection or rebellion against the United States, or any claim for the loss or emancipation of any slave; but all such debts, obligations, and claims shall be held illegal and void.

Section 5. The Congress shall have power to enforce, by appropriate legislation, the provisions of this article.

[Declared in force, July 23, 1868.]

ARTICLE XV

Section 1. The right of the citizens of the United States to vote shall not be denied or abridged by the United States or by any state, on account of race, color, or previous condition of servitude.

Section 2. The Congress shall have power to enforce this article by appropriate legislation.

[Declared in force, March 30, 1870.]

ARTICLE XVI

The Congress shall have power to lay and collect taxes on incomes, from whatever source derived, without apportionment among the several states, and without regard to any census or enumeration.

[Declared in force, February 25, 1913.]

ARTICLE XVII

The Senate of the United States shall be composed of two senators from each state, elected by the people thereof for six years; and each senator shall have one vote. The electors in each state shall have the qualifications requisite for electors of the most numerous branch of the state legislatures.

When vacancies happen in the representation of any state in the senate, the executive authority of such state shall issue writs of election to fill such vacancies; provided, that the legislature of any state may empower the executive thereof to make temporary appointments until the people fill the vacancies by election as the legislature may direct.

This amendment shall not be so construed as to affect the election or term of any senator chosen before it becomes valid as part of the Constitution.

[Declared in force, May 31, 1913.]

ARTICLE XVIII

Section 1. After one year from the ratification of this article the manufacture, sale, or transportation of intoxicating liquors within, the importation thereof into, or exportation thereof from the United States and all territory subject to the jurisdiction thereof, for beverage purposes is hereby prohibited.

Section 2. The Congress and the several states shall have concurrent power to enforce this article by appropriate legislation.

Section 3. This article shall be inoperative unless it shall have been ratified as an amendment to the Constitution by the legislatures of the several states, as provided in the Constitution, within seven years from the date of submission hereof to the states by the Congress.

[Declared in force, January 29, 1919; repealed by Twenty-first Amendment.]

ARTICLE XIX

The right of the citizens of the United States to vote shall not be denied or abridged by the United States or by any state on account of sex.

Congress shall have power to enforce this article by appropriate legislation.

[Declared in force, August 26, 1920.]

ARTICLE XX

Section 1. The terms of the President and Vice-President shall end at noon on the 20th day of January, and the terms of senators and representatives at noon on the 3rd day of January, of the years in which such terms would have ended if this article had not been ratified; and the terms of their successors shall then begin.

Section 2. The Congress shall assemble at least once in every year, and such meeting shall begin at noon on the 3rd day of January, unless they shall by law appoint a different day.

Section 3. If, at the time fixed for the beginning of the term of President, the President elect shall have died, the Vice-President elect shall become President. If a President shall not have been chosen before the time fixed for the beginning of his term, or if the President elect shall have failed to qualify, then the Vice-President elect shall act as President until a President shall have qualified; and the Congress may by law provide for the case wherein neither a President elect nor a Vice-President elect shall have qualified, declaring who shall then act as President, or the manner in which one who is to act shall be selected, and such person shall act accordingly until a President or Vice-President shall have qualified.

Section 4. The Congress may by law provide for the case of the death of any of the persons from whom the House of Representatives may choose a President, whenever the right of choice shall have devolved upon them, and for the case of the death of any of the persons from whom the Senate may choose a Vice-President, whenever the right of choice shall have devolved upon them.

Section 5. Sections 1 and 2 shall take effect on the 15th day of October following the ratification of this article.

Section 6. This article shall be inoperative unless it shall have been ratified as an amendment to the Constitution by the legislatures of three-fourths of the several states within seven years from the date of its submission.

[Declared in force, February 6, 1933.]

ARTICLE XXI

Section 1. The eighteenth article of amendment to the Constitution of the United States is hereby repealed.

Section 2. The transportation or importation into any state, territory, or possession of the United States, for delivery or use therein of intoxicating liquors, in violation of the laws thereof, is hereby prohibited.

Section 3. This article shall be inoperative unless it shall have been ratified as an amendment to the Constitution by conventions in the several states, as provided in the Constitution, within seven years from the date of the submission hereof to the states by the Congress.

[Declared in force, December 5, 1933.]

ARTICLE XXII

No person shall be elected to the office of the President more than twice, and no person who has held the office of President, or acted as President, for more than two years of a term to which some other person was elected President shall be elected to the office of the President more than once. But this article shall not apply to any person holding the office of President when this article was proposed by the Congress, and shall not prevent any person who may be holding the office of President, or acting as President, during the term within which this article becomes operative from holding the office of President or acting as President during the remainder of such term.

[Declared in force, February 26, 1951.]

ARTICLE XXIII

Section 1. The District constituting the seat of government of the United States shall appoint in such manner as the Congress may direct: A number of electors of President and Vice-President equal to the whole number of senators and representatives in Congress to which the District would be entitled if it were a state, but in no event more than the least populous state; they shall be in addition to those appointed by the states, but they shall be considered, for the purposes of the election of President and Vice-President, to be electors appointed by a state; and they shall meet in the District and perform such duties as provided by the twelfth article of amendment.

Section 2. The Congress shall have power to enforce this article by appropriate legislation.

[Declared in force, April 3, 1961.]

ARTICLE XXIV

Section 1. The right of citizens of the United States to vote in any primary or other election for President or Vice-President, for electors for President or Vice-President, or for Senator or Representative in Congress, shall not be denied or abridged by the United States or any state by reason of failure to pay any poll tax or other tax.

Section 2. The Congress shall have the power to enforce this article by appropriate legislation.

[Declared in force, January 23, 1964.]

ARTICLE XXV

Section 1. In case of the removal of the President from office or his death or resignation, the Vice-President shall become President.

Section 2. Whenever there is a vacancy in the office of the Vice-President, the President shall nominate a Vice-President who shall take the office upon confirmation by a majority vote of both houses of Congress.

Section 3. Whenever the President transmits to the President pro tempore of the Senate and the Speaker of the House of Representatives his written declaration that he is unable to discharge the powers and duties of his office, and until he transmits to them a written declaration to the contrary, such powers and duties shall be discharged by the Vice-President as Acting President.

Section 4. Whenever the Vice-President and a majority of either the principal officers of the executive departments or of such other body as Congress may by law provide, transmit to the President pro tempore of the Senate and the Speaker of the House of Representatives their written declaration that the President is unable to discharge the powers and duties of his office, the Vice-President shall immediately assume the powers and duties of the office as Acting President.

Thereafter, when the President transmits to the President pro tempore of the Senate and the Speaker of the House of Representatives his written declaration that no inability exists, he shall resume the powers and duties of his office unless the Vice-President and a majority of either the principal officers of the executive department or of such other body as Congress may by law provide, transmit within four days to the President pro tempore of the Senate and the Speaker of the House of Representatives their written declaration that the President is unable to discharge the powers and duties of his office. Thereupon Congress shall decide the issue, assembling within 48 hours for that purpose if not in session. If the Congress, within 21 days after receipt of the latter written declaration, or, if Congress is not in session, within 21 days after Congress is required to assemble, determines by two-thirds vote of both houses that the President is unable to discharge the powers and duties of his office, the Vice-President shall continue to discharge the same as Acting President; otherwise, the President shall resume the powers and duties of his office.

Notes

Suggestions for
Additional Reading

Index

Notes

1. Questions are taken from the American Civil Liberties Union brochure *Where Do You Stand? Twenty Questions on Civil Liberties* (American Civil Liberties Union, 156 Fifth Avenue, New York, N.Y. 10010, October 1966).
2. William O. Douglas, *A Living Bill of Rights* (New York: Doubleday & Company, Inc., 1961), p. 16.
3. Alpheus T. Mason, *The Supreme Court in a Free Society* (Englewood Cliffs, N.J.: Prentice-Hall, Inc., 1959), pp. 157–159.
4. As of July 1, 1967, the Supreme Court membership included Hugo Black, F. D. R., 1937; William Douglas, F. D. R., 1939; Earl Warren (Chief Justice), Eisenhower, 1953; John Harlan, Eisenhower, 1955; William Brennan, Eisenhower, 1956; Potter Stewart, Eisenhower, 1958; Byron White, Kennedy, 1962; Abe Fortas, Johnson, 1965; Thurgood Marshall, Johnson, 1967.
5. Robert C. Weaver, *The Urban Complex* (New York: Doubleday & Company, Inc., 1964), p. 1.
6. R. C. Weaver, *op. cit.,* p. 38.
7. William O. Douglas, *America Challenged* (New York: Avon Books, 1960), p. 32.

8. Clark Kerr, "The Exaggerated Generation," *The New York Times Magazine,* June 4, 1967, p. 28.

9. Claude L. Heathcock, *The United States Constitution in Perspective* (Boston: Allyn and Bacon, 1964), pp. 265–266.

10. Anthony Lewis, *Portrait of a Decade* (New York: Random House, Inc., 1964), p. 19.

11. Anthony Lewis, *op. cit.,* p. 29.

12. Fred P. Graham, *The New York Times,* May 15, 1967, p. 1.

13. Judge Harold R. Medina, Introduction to *Liberty under Law* (Columbus: American Educational Publishers, Inc., 1963), p. 4.

14. *ACLU News Release,* The American Civil Liberties Union, New York, New York, May 5, 1967.

15. *Ibid.*

16. *The New York Times,* Aug. 9, 1967, p. 20.

17. Fred M. Hechinger, *The New York Times,* October 16, 1966, p. 11.

18. *Ibid.*

19. *Ibid.*

20. Donald Parker and others, *Civil Liberties* (Boston: Houghton Mifflin Company, 1965), p. xiii.

21. Board of Education, City of New York, *Curriculum Bulletin No. 4,* 1964–1965 series, pp. 147–148.

22. *Facts on File Yearbook, 1965* (New York: Facts on File, Inc., August 5–11, 1965), p. 286.

23. William Brink and Louis Harris, *The Negro Revolution in America* (New York: Simon & Schuster, 1964), p. 164.

24. *Ibid.*

Suggestions for Additional Reading

1. CBS NEWS, *The National Citizenship Test*. New York, Bantam Books, 1965. This paperback based upon a series of TV programs asks and answers many vital questions dealing with the rights and responsibilities of U.S. citizens.

2. DOUGLAS, WILLIAM O., *Freedom of the Mind*. New York, American Library Association in cooperation with the Public Affairs Committee, Inc., 1962. Justice Douglas here discusses some of the basic problems of civil rights such as the trend to conformity, libel law, and loyalty oaths. Included also is an annotated bibliography.

3. HANDLIN, OSCAR, *Fire Bell in the Night—The Crisis*. New York, Little, Brown Company, 1964. This is a brief but detailed description of some of the basic problems facing the U.S. in regard to the isolation of the Negro and the current surfacing of racism in the United States outside of the South.

4. HANNA, JOHN PAUL, *Teenagers and the Law*. Boston, Ginn and Company, 1967. This little book describes selected aspects of law as it applies to American youth.

5. *Judgment Series,* Washington, D.C., Civic Education Service, 1733 K Street N.W., Washington, D.C. 20006. This is a series of pamphlets published originally by the National Council for the Social Studies. Each case in the series includes a detailed analysis of some of the most controversial Supreme Court decisions.

6. *National Advisory Commission on Civil Disorders, Report,* with special Introduction by Tom Wicker. New York, Bantam Books, 1968. This is the famous report of the U.S. Riot Commission, a special committee appointed by President Johnson to investigate the causes of riots in the cities. The committee went beyond the mandate of the President to discuss backgrounds, conditions, and historical circumstances which led to the riots.

7. ROCHE, JOHN P., *The Quest for the Dream*. New York, The Macmillan Company, 1963. This book was published as the fiftieth anniversary book of the Anti-Defamation League. It presents in a vivid historical development the battles for civil and human rights.

8. STEVENS, WILLIAM O., *Footsteps to Freedom.* New York, Dodd, Mead & Company, Inc., 1954. This is an account written for young people of the development of political freedom from ancient times to the present.

9. *Freedom Now! The Civil Rights Struggle in America,* Westin, Alan F., ed. New York, Basic Books, Inc., 1964. This is an excellent anthology of articles by prominent Americans engaged in the battle for civil rights. Primary emphasis is placed on the plight of the American Negro.

Index

A. Philip Randolph Institute, 102

Abernathy, Ralph, 38

Aberrations, 90

Absolute despotism, 61

ACLU (*see* American Civil Liberties Union)

Affidavit, 84

American Civil Liberties Union (ACLU), 21, 46
and right to wear long hair in public schools, 88-94

Anniston, Alabama, 127-28

Appellate jurisdiction, of Supreme Court, 26

Appellate review, 136

Arbitrary arrest, 140

Arkansas, school desegregation in Little Rock, 119-25

Arms, right to keep and bear, 67

Ashbee, Lewis, 90

Athens, Georgia, 127

Atlanta, Georgia, 127

Augusta, Georgia, 127

Avondale (Cincinnati), 30

Backlash, white, 39

Baez, Joan, *(fig.)* 105

Bail, defined, 70*n.*

Baker, Russell, 93

Baron, Kay, 119-25

Batesville, Mississippi, voter registration in, *(fig.)* 73

Bill of Rights, 21-22
and Fourteenth Amendment, 79*n.*
interpretation of, by Warren Court, 25-28
and rights of youth, 40-42, 44
text of, 163-65, *(fig.)* 68

Bills of attainder, 22-23, 62*n.*

Birmingham, Alabama, 127-29

Black, Hugo:
on protection of civil rights and liberties, 25
on school prayers, and religious freedom, 78-82

Black power, 32
as means to integration, 55
and race riots, 107-108

Board of Education (New York State), 85-87

Board of Regents (New York State), and school prayers, 78-82

Bond, Julian, 38

Brandeis, Louis D., 91, 94

Brennan, William J., Jr., on civil liberties, 49-50

Brink, William, 55

Brown, H. Rap, 38

Brown, Henry Billings, on race relations, 36-37

Brown, Minnijean, 119-25

Brown v. Board of Education of Topeka, Kansas (1954), 26, 36, 115-18

Capital crime, 69

Carmichael, Stokely, 38

Census Bureau (U.S.), 28

Charlotte, North Carolina, 126

Cheating, and punishment of minors, 83-87

China, Communist, 94

Cincinnati, Ohio, ghettos in, 30

Cities:
minority group immigration to, 28-31
tension in, 30-31

Civil disobedience, 102-106

Civil liberties:
and civil rights, 17-55
Constitution of U.S. as basis for, 21-25
problems of determining, 17-20
role of Supreme Court in determining, 25-28
text of Constitution pertaining to, 62-66

Civil rights:
and civil liberties, 17-55
Constitution of U.S. as basis for, 21-25
effect of movement for, on Negro revolution, 33-41

effectiveness of laws, 50-55
influence of urbanization on, 28-31
influence of youth on, 31-33
laws for, and prejudice, 53-55
and long hair, 47-50
Negro struggle for, 30-31
problems of determining, 17-20
role of Supreme Court in determining, 25-28
text of Constitution pertaining to, 62-66

Civil Rights Act (1964), 130-36
provisions of, 51-52

Civil Rights Commission, 52, 133-34, 135

Cleveland, Ohio:
ghettos in, 30
National Guard quelling riot in, *(fig.)* 70

Coffin, William S., Jr., *(fig.)* 98

Collusion, 99

Commerce, U.S. Department of, 52, 136

Committee for a Sane Nuclear Policy (SANE), *(fig.)* 43

Common law, 70

Communists, rights of, and Supreme Court, 25

Community Relations Service (of Commerce Department), 136

Competency, 113

Competent national tribunals, 140

Conciliate, 136

Confessions, forced:
of minors, 85
Supreme Court on, 25-26
Congress of Racial Equality
(CORE), 31, 38, 129
Constitution (of United
States):
amendments to, 163-75
as basis of civil rights and
liberties, 21-25
interpretation of, by Warren
Court, 25-28
selected amendments of,
67-74
signers of, 161-62
text of, 145-61
text of, relating to civil
rights and liberties, 62-66
CORE (see Congress of
Racial Equality)
Counsel, right to, 75-77
Counter-violence, 110
Court of Appeals for the
Second Circuit (United
States), and draft-card
burning, 46
Courts:
under Civil Rights Act
(1964), 136
juvenile, and Supreme
Court, 40-42
Coxe, Spencer, 88-94
Crimes against humanity, 97-
98
Criminal contempt, 136

Danville, Virginia, 126
De facto segregation, (figs.)
20, 51
Declaration of Independence,
59-61, 131, (fig.) 60
Democracy:

civil rights and liberties in,
17-20
and loyal opposition, 94
Demonstrations, 38, 43, (figs.)
32, 93, 96, 135
Despotism, absolute, 61
Detention, 140
Detroit, Michigan, race riots
in (1967), 107
District of Columbia, school
segregation in, 114
Douglas, William O., on
revolt, 31
Draft, advertisement urging
resistance to, 95-101
Draft registration card, 44
Draft-card burners, treatment
of by courts, 44-46

Eavesdropping, electronic,
(fig.) 21
Eckford, Elizabeth, (fig.) 120
Education, public:
and determining civil liberties, 17
as means to integrated
society, 55
and "separate but equal"
doctrine, 36-38
Eighth Amendment, text of,
70-72
Eisenhower, Dwight D., 26,
119
Electors, 74n.
Employment, under Civil
Rights Act (1964), 134-
35
Engle v. Vitale, Jr. (1962),
78-82
Englewood, New Jersey, de
facto segregation in
schools of, (fig.) 20

Equal Protection Clause (of Fourteenth Amendment), 23

Evans, Jacqueline F., *(fig.)* 122

Evers, Medgar, 38

Ex-post facto laws, 22, 62n.

Fabricant, Neil, 86

Farmer, James, 38

Federal aid, under Civil Rights Act (1964), 134

Fifteenth Amendment, 23
and right to vote, 23
text of, 72

Fifth Amendment:
and cheating by minors, 84
and public schools, 49
text of, 69

First Amendment:
and draft resistance, 46, 100
and right to wear long hair in public schools, 88
and school prayer issue, 79
text of, 67

Florida:
and *Gideon v. Wainright* (1963), 75-77
Supreme Court of, 77

Flushing, New York, cheating case in, 83-87

Fortas, Abe, on rights of juveniles in courts, 42

Fourteenth Amendment, 112-18
and Bill of Rights, 79
citizenship guarantees of, 23
text of, 72

Fourth Amendment:
electronic eavesdropping as violation of, *(fig.)* 21

text of, 69

Fox, Joseph, 119-25

Freedom, Constitutional guarantees of, 22-23

Freedom riders, *(fig.)* 134
bomb tossed into bus of, *(fig.)* 123
diary of, 126-29

"Freedom School," children attending, *(fig.)* 51

Geneva Accord (1954), 97

Geneva Conventions (1949), 98

Ghettos, 28-30

Gideon, Clarence Earl, 75-77

Gideon v. Wainright (1963), 75-77

Goodman, Mitchell, *(fig.)* 98

Grand jury, 69n.

Great Society, 33

Green, Ernest, 119-25

Grievances, redress of, 67

Habeas corpus, writ of, 22, 62n.

Harlan, John Marshall, on race relations, 37

Harlem (New York), 30

Harris, David, 90

Harris, Louis, 55

Hartford, Connecticut, riot in, 107

Hechinger, Fred, 48-49

Hillside, New Jersey, 47

Holtzman, Lester, 83, 86

Hough (Cleveland), 30

Immunities, 72

Impartial tribunal, 140

Impeachment, 63

"In loco parentis" theory, in public schools, 48

Indians (American), 33

Indictment, 77

  by a Grand Jury, 69

Integration:

  "black power" as means to, 55

  education as means to, 55

  of public schools, (fig.) 116

Internal combustion, 107n.

Intrastate passengers, defined, 127n.

Johnson, Lyndon B., 26, 130

  on passage of Voting Rights Act (1965), 52-53

Judicial power, 63

Jurisdiction:

  appellate, of Supreme Court, 26

  original, of Supreme Court, 26

Jury trial, right to, 63, 69, 70

Justice, U.S. Department of, 127

Juvenile courts, and Supreme Court, 40-42

Kennedy, John F., 26, 33, 80

  on need for civil rights legislation, 50

Kennedy, Robert F., 129

Kerr, Clark, on protest movements, 32-33

King, Martin Luther, Jr., 38

Laws:

  for civil rights, and prejudice, 53-55

  violations of, by youths, 40-44

Lewis, Anthony, 119-25

Limbo, 86

Lincoln, Abraham, 52

Lindsay, John V., 110

Little Rock, Arkansas:

  school desegregation in, 119-25

  student reaction to school desegregation in, 119-25

Lomax, Louis E., 126-29

Long hair:

  right to wear, 47-50

  wearing of, in public schools, 88-94

Los Angeles, ghettos in, 30

Louisiana:

  law of, and Plessy v. Ferguson (1896), 36-37

  "separate but equal" facilities in, 112

Loyalty oaths, rights of those refusing to sign, and Supreme Court, 25

McKissick, Floyd, 38

Magna Carta, defined, 131n.

Majority will, and rights and liberties of minority groups in a democracy, 17-20

March on Washington (1963), (fig.) 133

Marshall, John, 25, 80

Marshall, Thurgood, 26-27

Medina, Harold R., on rights and responsibilities of youth, 43-44

Meredith, James, 38

Mexican-Americans, immigration of, 28-29

Minority groups:

  population of, in United States, 28-29

rights and liberties of, in a democratic society, 17-20

Misdemeanor, 85

Mississippi, voter registration in Batesville, *(fig.)* 73

Montgomery, Alabama, 129

NAACP (*see* National Association for the Advancement of Colored People)

National Association for the Advancement of Colored People (NAACP), 38

National Day of Prayer, 82

National Guard, during race riot in Cleveland, Ohio, *(fig.)* 70

Nazis, 94

Negro ghettos, 30

Negro revolution, effect of civil rights movement on, 33-41

Negro Revolution in America (Brink and Harris), 55

Negroes:
civil rights struggle of, 30-31
compensation of, 39
immigration of, 28-29
population of, in United States, 29, 33
rights of, and Supreme Court, 25

New Frontier, 33

New Jersey:
de facto segregation in Englewood schools, *(fig.)* 20
race riots in Newark (1967), 107-11, *(fig.)* 109
suspension of student wearing skullcap by school in Hillside, 47

New Jersey State Commissioner of Education, 47

New Left, 32

New Orleans, Louisiana, 126, 129

New York City, ghettos in, 30

New York Civil Liberties Union:
and draft-card burners, 46
and punishment for cheating, 86
and students' right to wear long hair, 47

New York State Board of Education, 85-87

New York State Board of Regents:
cheating on Regents examination, 83-87
and school prayers, 78-82

New York State Commissioner of Education, 47

New York Times, The:
on appointment of Thurgood Marshall to Supreme Court, 26-27
on juvenile courts, 42
on race riots in American cities, 107-11
on school desegregation in Little Rock, 119-25
summary of Civil Rights Act (1964), 130-36
on suspension of students with long hair, 47-49

Newark, New Jersey, race riots in (1967), 107-11, *(fig.)* 109

Nineteenth Amendment:
text of, 72-73
and women's right to vote, 23, *(fig.)* 24

Ninth Amendment, text of, 72

Norwalk, Connecticut, and long hair issue, *(fig.)* 48

Nuremberg, Germany, 98

"Official religion," 79-80

Original jurisdiction, of Supreme Court, 26

Palliatives, 110

Panama City, Florida, 75

Parker, Sammy Dean, 119-25

Patterson, John A., 129

Peace Corps, 33

Pelletreau, Francis, *(fig.)* 89

Pennsylvania, school law in, 88-89

Pledge of Allegiance to the Flag, and religion, 82

Plessy v. Ferguson (1896), 36-37, 112-15, 116

Poll tax, 74

Poor people, and right to court-appointed lawyers, 75-77

Population, of United States, 28-29

Poverty, war on, 33

Prayers, in public schools, and religious freedom, 78-82

Prejudice, and civil rights laws, 53-55

Primary election, 73

Privacy, right to, 91

Prosecute, 76

Public accommodation, under Civil Rights Act (1964), 132

Public facilities, under Civil Rights Act (1964), 132-33

Puerto Ricans, immigration of, 28-29

Race relations, Supreme Court view of, 36-38

Racial intermarriage, 113

Racism, 55

Randolph, A. Philip, 38

Rebuttable presumption, 131

Red Guards, 94

Registrars, 131

Relief to plaintiff, 115

Religious freedom:
  and draft resistance, 98-99
  and school prayers, 78-82
  violation of, 47

Remanding back to court, 77

RESIST, 95-101

Resistance, to authority, 95-101

Revolt:
  William O. Douglas on, 31
  of youth in U.S., 31-33, *(fig.)* 32

Ricketts, Mrs. 119-25

Rights, unalienable, 59

Riots, racial, 107-11
  National Guard during, *(fig.)* 70
  prevention of, 40

Rock Hill, South Carolina, 127

Roosevelt, Franklin D., 26

Running amok, 110

Rustin, Bayard, 38, 102-06

Sabbatical leave, 84

San Francisco, California, 90

Sanctioning official prayers, 78

SANE (*see* Committee for a Sane Nuclear Policy)

Schanberg, Sydney H., 83-87

School prayers, and religious freedom, 78-82

Schools, public:
  under Civil Rights Act (1964), 133
  de facto segregation in, of Englewood, New Jersey, *(fig.)* 20
  and *"in loco parentis"* theory, 48
  segregation in, and Supreme Court, 26
  student suspension by, for long hair, 47-50, 88-94

SCLC (*see* Southern Christian Leadership Conference)

SDS (*see* Students for a Democratic Society)

Second Amendment, text of, 67

Segregation, 39
  de facto, 20, 51
  legal (1896-1954), 36
  in public schools, 24, 26, 114-17

Selective Service Act, 1965 amendment to, 46

Selective Service System, 44

Self-expression, right to, 91-92

"Separate but equal" doctrine, 36-37, 112-18

Seventh Amendment, text of, 70

Shuttlesworth, Fred, 38

Sixth Amendment, text of, 69-70

Slavery, prohibition of, 23, 72

SNCC (*see* Student Nonviolent Coordinating Committee)

Southern Christian Leadership Conference (SCLC), 32, 38

Spock, Benjamin, *(fig.)* 98

"Star-Spangled Banner," and religion, 81

Stewart, Potter, 42
  on school prayer issue, 79-82

Student Nonviolent Coordinating Committee (SNCC), 31-32, 38

Students for a Democratic Society (SDS), 32

Supreme Court (Florida), and *Gideon v. Wainright* (1963), 77

Supreme Court (Queens, New York), 83

Supreme Court (United States:
  appointment of justices to, 27-28
  and *Brown v. Board of Education of Topeka, Kansas* (1954), 36
  composition of, 26-27, *(fig.)* 27
  and draft-card burners, 44
  and *Engle v. Vitale, Jr.* (1965), 78-82
  and *Gideon v. Wainright* (1963), 75-77
  interpretation of Constitution by, and social climate, 28
  jurisdiction of, 26
  and juvenile courts, 40-42
  and right to wear long hair in public schools, 92
  role of, in defining civil rights and liberties, 25-28

and segregation in public schools, 26

and "separate but equal" doctrine, 112-18

Sutherland, George, 77

Tampa, Florida, ghettos in, 30

Tenth Amendment, text of, 72

Third Amendment, text of, 69

Thirteenth Amendment:
  and slavery, 23
  text of, 72

Transient causes, 61

Treason, 63

Trial by jury, right to, 63, 69, 70

Twenty-fourth Amendment:
  and poll taxes, 23
  text of, 73-74

Unalienable rights, 59

United Nations, 96, 138-40

United States:
  minority groups in, 28-29, 33
  Negro population of, 29, 33
  population of, 28-29
  Vietnam policy of, and draft-card burners, 44-46

Universal Declaration of Human Rights (United Nations), 138-40

Urban League, 38

Urbanization, influence of, on civil rights, 28-31

Usurpations, 61

Vietnam, war in, and draft resistance, 44-46, 95-101

Violence, prevention of, 39-40

Voting:
  under Civil Rights Act (1964), 131
  prohibition of poll tax as qualification for, 23
  right of, 23, 72-73
  women's right of, 23, *(fig.)* 24

Voting Rights Act (1965), 51-52

War on poverty, 33

Warrants, 69

Warren, Earl, 25, 37

Washington, D.C., 126

Washington, George, 80

Watts (Los Angeles), 30
  race riots in (1965), 107

Weaver, Robert C., 29

White backlash, 39

White establishment, 110

Wilkins, Roy, 38

Winnsboro, South Carolina, 127

Women, voting rights of, 23, *(fig.)* 24

Woods, Robin, 119-25

Ybor City (Tampa), 30

Young, Whitney, 38

Youth:
  as civil rights demonstrators, *(fig.)* 32
  influence of, on civil rights, 31-33
  safeguarding rights of, 40-44
  in revolt, 31-33 *(fig.)* 32
  violation of laws by, 40-44